Storying Learning
in Early Childhood

Rethinking Childhood

Gaile S. Cannella
General Editor

Vol. 54

The Rethinking Childhood series is part of the Peter Lang Education list.
Every volume is peer reviewed and meets
the highest quality standards for content and production.

PETER LANG
New York • Bern • Frankfurt • Berlin
Brussels • Vienna • Oxford • Warsaw

Elizabeth P. Quintero

Storying Learning in Early Childhood

When Children Lead Participatory Curriculum Design, Implementation, and Assessment

PETER LANG
New York • Bern • Frankfurt • Berlin
Brussels • Vienna • Oxford • Warsaw

KH

Library of Congress Cataloging-in-Publication Data

Quintero, Elizabeth P.
Storying learning in early childhood: when children lead participatory curriculum
design, implementation, and assessment / Elizabeth P. Quintero.
pages cm. — (Rethinking childhood; v. 54)
Includes bibliographical references.
1. Early childhood education—United States. 2. Early childhood education—Curricula—
United States. 3. Student participation in curriculum planning—United States.
4. Student-centered learning—United States. 5. Storytelling. I. Title.
LB1139.25.Q85   372.210973—dc23   2015014869
ISBN 978-1-4331-2748-9 (hardcover)
ISBN 978-1-4331-2747-2 (paperback)
ISBN 978-1-4539-1566-0 (e-book)
ISSN 1086-7155

Bibliographic information published by **Die Deutsche Nationalbibliothek**.
Die Deutsche Nationalbibliothek lists this publication in the "Deutsche
Nationalbibliografie"; detailed bibliographic data are available
on the Internet at http://dnb.d-nb.de/.

The paper in this book meets the guidelines for permanence and durability
of the Committee on Production Guidelines for Book Longevity
of the Council of Library Resources.

© 2015 Peter Lang Publishing, Inc., New York
29 Broadway, 18th floor, New York, NY 10006
www.peterlang.com

Printed in the United States of America

5/9/16

CONTENTS

Chapter 1. Introduction: What Is and What Could Be...   1

Chapter 2. Curriculum in Early Childhood: A Complicated
               Conversation Among University Teacher
               Education Students   25

Chapter 3. Complicated Conversations: What We're Learning
               About Integrated Curriculum   49

Chapter 4. Assessment in Early Childhood: Storying Learning   75

Chapter 5. Early Childhood Issues: An Understatement   95

Chapter 6. What Are Childcare Markets and How Are Measures
               of Quality Related to Funding?   113

Chapter 7. Through the Lens of Migrant Families   129

Chapter 8. What Could Be...   147

· 1 ·

INTRODUCTION: WHAT IS AND WHAT COULD BE...

While it is encouraging that, in the United States and internationally, early care and education is becoming a frequent topic of conversation in policy and political discussions, we still have a long way to go. There is a vast lack of knowledge about the intricacies of early care and education in most arenas, and not much agreement on how to carry out the complex job of actual implementation. How may I paint a picture of the realities of our current world in early childhood studies in 2015? There is evidence that shows:

(1) a dramatic lack of learner-centered curricula that is experientially, culturally, and linguistically responsive, or that considers the meaning-making participation of children with peers, adults, things, and places;

(2) inappropriate standardized assessment;

(3) inadequate teacher preparation and access to professional study in the field; and

(4) nonexistent measures to ensure equity and funding for the youngest of learners. (Iorio & Adler, 2013; Quintero, 2010; Steinberg & Kincheloe, 2009)

And why does this matter? There are many reasons we should tune in to these realities. Probably the best two reasons that most readers will agree with are that we can do better, and that children are depending on us to do so.

The research described in this book documents a combination of philosophy, research, and critical questions about notions of child development that still heavily influence the profession, and examples of the learning potential of all children through their human relationships and their experiences. Through an ongoing 5-year qualitative study, we focused on the contexts of homes, schools, and communities, and critically created child-centered curriculum, and assessment collaborations. Families, children, and their teachers contributed unending support and a treasure trove of ideas. And this work that crosses boundaries of home, school, and community brought into focus policy issues, economic issues, and political realities that affect us all as we engage in curriculum and assessment. We have barriers and opportunities.

And of course, this qualitative study found both expected and unexpected connections among complicated issues about early care and education that have been raised for years. One intention of presenting the findings here is to fuel our ongoing conversations. The work here offers some specific examples of the possibilities that can be realized when children, families, and early childhood professionals collaborate, take risks, and support each other and participate.

Meet Melina

An early childhood studies student teacher that had worked as an early childhood teacher for a number of years related a story and raised some questions about the potential of children, and the curriculum and the assessment that could really support all children. She explained,

I will name the child whose story I tell Melina;[1] she came to our center not too long ago. She is 4 years of age and is very social and enjoys having conversations with me. Melina is always willing to participate in many of the activities available in the classroom. In our classroom we have been talking about families and what families do at work. I had finished reading a book about families and Melina invited me to play with her. She and I were playing with geometric shapes at the manipulatives table. I found several "house-shaped" manipulatives and I lined them up, then around the houses

I placed some green triangle shaped-manipulatives. The following conversation occurred between us:

Melina:	Teacher Angie, what are you doing?
Me:	I'm building a house and around the house I have planted several tall trees.
Melina:	That looks like my house in Mexico. I have lots of trees around my house in Mexico (she looks at my design and smiles).
Me:	Melina, I see you have a building, too; tell me about your structure. (She has a line of 6 triangles and between she has inserted hexagons, then around them she placed some blue trapezoids.)
Melina:	These are cows (she points to the triangles) and they are inside their house (pointing to the hexagons). These here are horses (she points to the trapezoids) and they are running everywhere.
Me:	Ah…I see. Do they live in Mexico?
Melina:	Yes! They live with my grandpa. My grandpa goes to the cows' houses and he gets the milk (she points out to the triangles). Look teacher, these are the cows, and my grandpa milks them like this (she holds her hands out in front of her and pretends to milk the cow). He goes to the cows' houses and gets the milk. (She points to the trapezoids.) These are the horses my grandpa has. He has lots of horses.
Me:	Ohh…Do the horses have houses, too?
Melina:	No! Teacher Angie, the horses like to run. He has lots and lots of horses. (Quintero, 2014, pp. 8–9)

The student teacher notes, "With Melina's story I can see that she has a vivid image of her hometown, her grandpa's ranch, and she is able to recreate her images through objects to tell her story" (Quintero, 2014). In our university class, we discussed all the "knowledge" and "skills" that this 4-year-old shows in an integrated, child-initiated activity. And we all asked, how can early childhood curricula provide opportunities for this type of learning, and how can early childhood assessments document this child's participation and potential?

Yoshikawa and colleagues (2013) compiled current research relating to the evidence base for quality early childhood programs for all children. Yet, it is still important to ask, how was it decided what "evidence" would be included in this "evidence base" (Dahlberg, Moss, & Pence, 2013)? And even with the expansive list of collaborators on this research compilation, is their collective view of "quality" meaningful for, and reflective of, families in our communities across the country and the world (Dahlberg et al., 2013)?

Recent public discussions buzz with excitement about recent neuroscientific research drawing a connection between the foundations of brain architecture as it supports lifelong learning potential being established in children's early years. For example, Yoshikawa et al. (2013) report,

> Early experiences in the home, in other care settings, and in communities interact with genes to shape the developing nature and quality of the brain's architecture. The growth and then environmentally based pruning of neuronal systems in the first years support a range of early skills, including cognitive (early language, literacy, math), social (theory of mind, empathy, prosocial), persistence, attention, and self-regulation and executive function skills (the voluntary control of attention and behavior). Later skills—in schooling and employment—build cumulatively upon these early skills. (p. 3)

Yet, some scholars in the field (to be discussed in Chapter 5) are seriously questioning the casual way many claims such as these are being used in our discussions and policy rationales. Furthermore, these skills and dispositions in their complexities, in the culturally layered and politically influenced societies, raise even more questions about which knowledge is valued in which contexts. Every day in our work with young children and families, the issues of strengths and needs of children and their families, and the diversity of contexts, demand that we continually question our definitions of what counts as "evidence" as we attempt to improve services. An additional brief excerpt from a case study dramatically illustrates this reality.

A Story of Juan, Environments, and Supportive Parents and Teachers

Mia, a site supervisor with many years teaching experience at a state-funded preschool program, told me the story of a boy we will call Juan. He was registered by his mother for this program in the large urban area in south central California in early September. He was 4 years old when he started school, and initially seemed happy to be there. However, his behavior, beginning with the first day and continuing for at least 3 weeks, was problematic in that he literally ran to a child or a group of children involved in play or work with materials, stayed less than 2 minutes, and then ran to a different group. He ran and ran, and no amount of gentle guidance about school routines and appropriate behaviors helped. The only time he seemed to settle in to doing anything with calm or interest was during outside playtime. In desperation, Mia took one set of materials from one of the indoor learning centers outside, and invited him to come outside with her to play. He did. He focused, talked with her as they played, and was a different child from the one who raced around the room indoors. So, the following day, the teachers put materials from several centers outside and gave all children the option to do the activities outdoors or indoors. This not only initiated a change in Juan's behaviors, it also began to change how the other children interacted with him. He began to make friends.

After a couple of weeks of this routine, the teachers began to bring back indoors the center activities, gradually—one each day. After a few weeks of this "change" back to an indoor classroom, Juan began to interact with his friends and teachers inside the classroom in meaningful ways.

At a home visit with his family in October, Mia learned some clues about the mystery of the child's initial interactions. She arrived at the home, and was greeted by the family. She found herself in a small, below-ground-level studio apartment with one small window (1' x 1') high on the bathroom wall. The mother apologized for the small space and explained that she and her husband and two children lived there with two other families. It was clear that when at home, Juan had no opportunity to look outdoors, or play outdoors, and only a few feet of space to play indoors (Quintero, 2014).

Context and evidence here are very different from what is often considered in discussions about developmental "milestones" guidelines and "ages and stages" timelines, yet the data are actually quite hopeful. The child himself negotiated his participation; the teachers were creative and took risks to support him and his family. This reveals a context of daily living that is more common (sadly) than we want to admit. The teachers' creative and authentically responsive ways to assess what may have been useful for the child, risk-taking to change their curriculum, and then investigating the child's living situation, certainly affected the way he was able to begin to participate fully in the early childhood program.

Who Are the Children Participating in Curriculum and Assessment?

It is old news that demographics are changing in communities, states, and nations all over the world. Migrating people bring cultural and linguistic histories, hopes and dreams for learning. They come from contexts in which every day brings struggle, and they join us to enroll their children in educational programs. An example of this is agricultural workers in our county in California, who include families from Mexico and Central America, and especially a large, close-knit, indigenous group of families from Oaxaca, Mexico, the Mixtecs. The Mixtecs are indigenous inhabitants of southern Mexico whose language and culture predate the Spanish conquest by hundreds of years. There are an estimated 500,000 Mixteco speakers today, almost one-fifth of whom live in the United States at least part of their lives (Fox & Rivera-Salgado, 2004). There are barriers for many of the Mixtec people living in California. Many are illiterate, and some speak neither Spanish nor English, but only their native language, Mixteco. As a result, they face exploitation and discrimination in labor, housing, and everyday life. Most live in extreme poverty and lack basic provisions such as adequate housing, food, clothing, and other necessities of life. Central to their struggle is the fact that they cannot communicate with people beyond their own indigenous community, thus impeding their ability to obtain appropriate health care, educate themselves and their children, negotiate with their employers to improve their work situations, and exercise their basic civil rights (Wright, 2005).

Some participants in the study for this book were early childhood studies student teachers working in programs throughout the county who became acquainted with Mixtec parents who are migrant farmworkers. Some parents had had some formal education in their home country, and some had had absolutely no formal education. Yet, the parents had knowledge and passionate determination about what they wanted for their children's education. Parents who were interviewed showed consensus in their responses to the question of what would be preferred language in early and general education for their children: "Bilingual English and Spanish, and another language if possible." Participants were also asked whether it is important that teachers understand or know of their home culture, and they answered, "Oh yes, because we all come from different cultures. For example, I am from Oaxaca and my culture is totally completely different from a person's culture from Michoacán and Guanajuato" (Quintero, 2012).

Considering these stories among millions just as complicated, it seems important to consider O'Laughlin's (2009) questions as we acknowledge our growing "evidence base" in the field:

> A minimal condition of depth pedagogy, therefore, is the reclamation of narrative threads and the location of children as subjects in history—people with genealogical filiations, narrative continuity, and a possibility for becoming that is informed by, but

not constrained by, ancestral, historical, and familial legacies. Each child possesses a culturally constituted unconscious that embodies ancestral history and ways of being, as well as inherited traumas due to displacements, wars, genocides, familial trauma, and other forms of unspoken and unmetabolized suffering. Ought not a teacher to be prepared to tap into these resources to help children better understand their locations in history? (pp. 40–41)

Not only must we be open to continually redefining evidence as it pertains to children's lives, but also O'Laughlin's comments point to the responsibility of professionals to continually strive to learn more through each interaction with children and families. This complexity of responsibility of responding to and respecting historical context in children's worlds is daunting; how are we preparing professionals, and how can this work be funded?

Funding Early Care and Education, and the Influence on Curriculum

In the past few years, joining the few lone economists acknowledging the importance of early care and education over the past 30 years, more economists are participating in the discussion about the urgency of providing early care and education. James Heckman, professor at the University of Chicago, has been promoting investment in early childhood education—financially and in terms of human capital. He brings in questions of research, quality, and curriculum regarding some of the research on Head Start programs and their effectiveness.

> There's a real problem with the way the evaluation study was conducted, and it's a very low quality program. If the quality of the program goes down, then you'd really have to be careful....I'm skeptical that you can get by on the cheap, really cheap, with Head Start. Head Start doesn't have one curriculum. Some Head Start programs are really using a version of Perry, maybe a diluted version. But others are using other curricula. So you wouldn't expect to see the same effects across these programs. The quality of inputs is lower. (quoted in Matthews, 2013)

Oh my. What does Heckman mean by "quality" here? Is he talking about the curriculum, the program itself, and/or the staff? Or is "quality" relating to the type of evaluation?

To those of us who have followed the longitudinal research beginning with the Perry Preschool Project every 5 years since the 1960s (Schweinhart,

Barnes, Weikart, Barnett, & Epstein, 1993), we hear information that we have considered for decades. With the revived discussion about the research and about various programs that have been implemented over the years, it is important to think about what is and what could be in 2015.

Chapters 5 and 6 of this book look deeper into the connection between differing societies' values and economic stances and the funding and estab-lishment of early care and education. It is important to note that Heckman and many other economists in the United States frame their thinking about early childhood funding rationales in terms of human capital and individual achievement. Children who have access to education will later become con-tributors to the national economy. What could be wrong with that? Well, what about children's well-being in terms of health, safety, shelter, and happi-ness during childhood and beyond? What about children's families' access to living situations that limit stress, both economic and emotional? What about children's opportunities to learn about collaboration and collective achieve-ments?

In addition to critical questions about the notion of human capital and individual achievement, we must also consider Heckman's work and the national political attention to the "achievement gap." More critical questions scream at us about "who is defining achievement?" and "how is this achieve-ment being measured"? And of course, who is responsible for children's access to early childhood programs so this "gap" doesn't happen? All the questions relate to curriculum and assessment, and beyond. Curriculum must be cul-turally, linguistically, and experientially responsive, integrated and research-based, and recursive, and must relate to pedagogy and to assessment. In the continuing discussion about *what is* the current state of affairs in early child-hood affairs, it is useful to consider *what could be*.

What Could Be: Curriculum and Assessment

Yoshikawa et al. (2013) present information that describes early childhood curricula which integrate curricula across domains (for example, socio-emotional and language; math and language), and which retain a feature of defined scope for each area. They (Yoshikawa et al.) note that "…in two recent successful instances, efforts were made to ensure feasible, integrated implementation; importantly, supporting coaches and mentor teachers were trained across the targeted domains and curricula" (2013, p. 9). Should it not trouble us that in the lexicon of education we still speak of teachers being "trained" (as an animal is "trained")? And furthermore, it is important to ask whether or not children and families are included in the decisions about targets, domains, and curricula.

Early childhood teacher education is about young children's learning, young children's learning to learn, and the social and cultural contexts where this learning takes place. It is also about the people and the human aspects that support this learning. It therefore requires an integrated approach to curriculum. And, finally, it is about an assessment system that documents the complicated process in such a way that data can be analyzed across settings so that we professionals may continually learn about the learning.

In the United States, we gasp with frustration and horror at each policy statement designed to "fix" education, "erase" the achievement gap, and "hold teachers and schools accountable." We know the measures outlined, however well-intentioned, will never work. Our certainty about our stance is for a variety of reasons and represented by our combined research and varied practice. It is tempting to identify each point of "Race to the Top," or each goal and objective from a politician's speech about early care and education, and slam the ideas for lack of research, lack of practicality, and their extreme potential for making matters worse. Yet, many in our field have begun to study and acknowledge with gratitude and interest the work of New Zealand early care and education researchers and teachers who designed and implemented a bicultural, bilingual curriculum and learning story assessment system. We are learning to adapt some of the critical, intellectual, academic, and practice-based structures that they have been using and perfecting for the past decades. These professionals have created a responsive (to children and families) and research-based curriculum and an assessment system that is linked foundationally and practically to the curriculum. With research in the study reported here in this book, we can provide examples of learning support that don't pit learners against each other as they traverse their educational journeys. Our models will not be continually subject to objectives and accountability measures set by top-down mandates, but will support collaborative and individual learning and document the journey in an authentic way.

The New Zealand researchers who created the learning story assessment model base their curriculum on learning dispositions, defined as "....complex units of educational input, uptake and outcome" (Carr, Duncan, Lee, Jones, Marshall, & Smith, 2009, p. 15). They say,

> We are more or less disposed to notice, recognize, respond to, reciprocate with, author, improvise from, and imagine alternatives to, what we already know and can do. (Carr et al., 2009, p. 15)

They address the importance of thinking about children's learning in all aspects of their lives:

> The cultures that develop in early childhood centres and school classrooms can be described as "dispositional milieux"; they may be overt and public, or subtle and covert; they may support the spirit and intent of a curriculum document or they may not…We suggest that learning dispositions are features of places, in the case of early childhood centres, school classrooms and homes. These dispositional milieux are affordance networks: networks of useful resources, including people, that provide, *or appear to provide*, opportunities and constraints for the learning that the individual has in mind. (Carr et al., 2009, p. 8)

Several Decades of Learning Context in Early Childhood From a Personal Lens

In terms of professional "history," the early childhood field is young. Certainly, early childhood professionals, in the past and currently, have learned much from the well-known scholars, philosophers, and practitioners of the past three centuries, including Jean-Jacques Rousseau, Johann Pestalozzi, Friedrich Froebel, Margaret Mahler, Lev Vygotsky, Jean Piaget, Maria Montessori, John Dewey, Lucy Sprague-Mitchell, and Magda Gerber, just to name a few. In the United States, since the mid-1960s and the inception of Head Start early care and education programs have become more numerous, more accessible (this is a relative term), and more complicated.

As a very green high school summer assistant in the 1960s, I spent days with a new Head Start teacher in rural Central Florida going to visit families (mostly African American descendants of sharecroppers) to disseminate information about the Head Start program that was opening in the area. I remember the smiling, engaged, and noticeably creative children of all ages acting out "stories" on the front porches or under a big oak tree. These experiences gave me a personal memory and context for information from Shirley Brice Heath's seminal work *Ways with Words: Language, Life and Work in Communities and Classrooms* (1983). Heath's work brought to the table a discussion of family culture, race, class, access, and issues of power in the world of early education.

In the early 1970s, I went to England. I spent every cent I had on a plane ticket because I wanted to visit the British infant schools[2] and Summerhill School[3] and study wherever I could. I found a program for preschool teachers, sponsored by the Greater London Authority, that involved classwork once a week and practical experience several days a week in inner-city neighborhood preschools. I was invited to participate in a school in a neighborhood of families who had migrated from the Middle East. During that year, I did observe British infant schools in the city, and visited Summerhill, and traveled to a school based on the Summerhill philosophy located in Castle Douglas, Scotland.

There, I saw evidence of very interesting child-centered education—that looked different from what my friends were experiencing in teacher education in the United States. One school had been in operation since the 1930s and the other was recently developed. The experiences gave me hope for better programs for young children.

I returned to the United States and continued to learn about working with children in both traditional and nontraditional settings. I observed the communication of monolingual English-speaking children, of African American children in both rural and inner-city schools, of monolingual Spanish-speaking children in Mexico, and of Spanish-English bilingual children in Texas and New Mexico. I saw literacy as an integral part of what children do as they understand and take part in their world. This was when Yetta Goodman and others—during the beginnings of the whole language movement— spoke of young children's play and communication as exemplifying the "roots of literacy." Literacy was spreading roots across and through the cultures of children in my world. I knew that I was witnessing the roots of *literacies*.

Children's self-initiated learning happens in many languages with similar passion, and with different sounds and strengths. During these times of observation and reflection about these developing literacies, I had the opportunity to work with many parents of young children as we collaborated on the task and pleasure of positively affecting the children's lives. Every parent I met—in a diversity of circumstances, from difficulty to comfort—cared deeply about his or her child entrusted to our care. Thus, I read with skepticism the research that implied that parents who lacked formal education would negatively affect the education of their children, because I had met numerous parents with only 3 to 5 years of formal schooling who had raised intelligent, successful children who are now attending the country's most prestigious universities (Quintero & Velarde, 1990).

The parents and many adults I met working with children had varying amounts of formal education and rich cultural histories, and they valued their daily work with children. They knew a lot that would be considered the "current state of knowledge." Yet, some of what they knew was clearly important knowledge for them and the children they worked with, but sometimes clashed with "knowledge in the field."

It happened that these were the years of the rollout of the *Developmentally Appropriate Practice Guidelines* by the National Association for the Education of Young Children (Bredekamp, 1987). The guidelines were a monumental event in the field of early childhood education that began the discussion about standards, best practices, and quality. And the debates continued across states, and even within communities in the same municipalities, regarding early childhood programs being responsive to families' wishes and aspirations. While it was good that our field of early childhood was attempting to document guidelines for practice to make suggestions for caregivers and teachers in the field who lacked academic and/or experiential background for this work, one size did not fit all. There is as much variety in the hopes and aspirations of families across and within our 50 states as there is in the people represented.

Questions that had arisen for me and others about the ethnocentricity and narrow approaches of the *Developmentally Appropriate Practice Guidelines*[4] led to activism by a group of early childhood people across the United States who participated with groups of children and families representing diverse cultural, linguistic, and economic backgrounds. We were angered by the focus of the professional dialogue on standards. And we were especially incensed by the discussions and the research designs, and flawed studies focusing on "at risk" children. We began our own small research projects, collaborating with children and families, which we renamed as "at promise." Some projects were written up in *Children and Families "at Promise": Deconstructing the Discourse of Risk* (Swadener & Lubeck, 1995.)

During this time, concerns arose in and outside the United States about whether these practices are sensitive to the needs of the various cultural communities in which they are enacted (Bloch, 1992, 2014; Grieshaber & Cannella, 2001). Brown and Lan (2015) state, "Even after two revisions (Bredekamp & Copple, 1997; Copple & Bredekamp, 2009), critics across the globe continue to argue there is an overdependence on developmental theory in DAP that tends to ignore the cultural and individual variations and differences found in these settings" (p. 1). Brown and Lan (2015) go on to explain that over the years, DAP has appeared to position Western developmental psychology as a stagnant body of research. In fact, organizations such as the American Psychological Association (2002) and the National Association of School Psychologists (Jones, 2009) frame their practices with children and families as an evolving process that increasingly takes into account the impact of culture on development.

Curriculum, Assessment, and More?

As stated earlier, early childhood teacher education is about young children's learning, young children's learning to learn, and the social and cultural contexts where this learning takes place. It is also about the people and the human aspects that support this learning. And, finally, it is about an assessment system that documents the complicated process in such a way that data can be analyzed across settings so that we professionals may continually learn about the learning.

Here in the United States, in California, politics, policy, and economics make it difficult for programs serving children and families. However, it is always wonderful for those of us who work with young children and have the joy of a seeing a child stand for the first time, share a dripping popsicle, and just laugh out loud at the bird in the window. For the professionals committed to providing the best possible educational situations for children and families, we are in the midst of policy and practice every day; both affect us, and we affect both.

After years of learning from children and families, and study about various theoretical and intellectual models that involve learning and teaching, I have seen that critical theory, critical literacy, and other postmodern frameworks with a dedication to acknowledging children's strengths as well as needs are the most positive and supportive ways to support early care and education for the children, their families, and their teachers and future teachers. As a New Zealand early childhood teacher educator said (Carr et al., 2009), "A curriculum is about the way we view the child." In addition, I am convinced that it is crucial to find an assessment strategy that brings families' "funds of knowledge" (Moll, Gonzalez, & Amanti, 2005) into the context of the learning communities in which we work.

Participants in this study and the work discussed in this book illustrate that, in a small way, we have begun to connect our work in teacher education to these "affordance networks" as a framework for encouraging our teacher education students, and all of us, to see ourselves as teacher researchers, curriculum developers, activity facilitators, evaluators of programs, and assessors of children's growth, development and learning. We see learning as a holistic connection that spirals and connects and reconnects in a variety of ways. The dynamic process and outcomes in our milieux teach us every day what we can improve upon, how much we all have yet to learn.

We believe it is urgent to be upfront in thinking about curriculum and assessment, and to ask important questions: Curriculum for whom? Assessment for whom? Sadly, many politicians, policy makers, and the general public believe that the 34% of students going home to speak a language other than English are a problem. Many of us in the field feel very strongly—and there is a huge body of research that supports our stance—that the children going home to speak other languages are an asset, not a problem or a liability. We acknowledge that for some teachers who have not been educated about teaching multilingual students, or for school districts whose funds are tied to test scores on tests that are not appropriate for dual-language learners, this is a problem—for them. The children are on their way to being multilingual, and if we only would take their lead, we could have a population of cognitively flexible, multilingual citizens. It is unacceptable that educated professionals in positions of power still perpetuate the misinformation that being multilingual is a problem.

Urban and rural neighborhoods and schools have increasing numbers of people representing ethnic, racial, and religious diversity. Many students today in schools around our country have exquisitely complex stories of going and coming. They have gone from home countries for a myriad of reasons, and they have come to their new country with a multitude of experiences. Many families in different parts of the United States have been living there for generations and still English is not their first or chosen language. Teachers and students can use native languages, personal story, and critical literacy as a way to enter neighborhoods and begin to learn from other stories of the various groups of people.

I remember from my work with immigrant and refugee families discussions with Hmong women describing their own childhoods in refugee camps in Thailand. Somali women described family life in East Africa during the past decades. I would say that the childhood experiences of these families are very different from those of many families in the United States, Western Europe, and many other regions. Brooker (interview, January 11, 2006) reports that Bangladeshi families in South London construct childhood in different ways than native British families do. Cannella (1997) believes that the knowledge base used to ground the field of early childhood education actually serves to support the status quo, reinforces prejudices and stereotypes, and ignores the real lives of children. Cannella's (1997) work has guided critical scholars by raising questions in terms of social justice and early education. Her questions include: How do we eliminate the two-tiered system? Does the curriculum respect the multiple knowledge and life experiences of younger human beings from diverse backgrounds? Sadly, we still are unsure how to effectively answer Cannella's questions. Katherine Nelson's work regarding new perspectives on development aims to delineate development that implies a less discussed "...role of evolution, representation, conceptual development, and the role of language in cognitive development, and different ideas about critical questions about...developmental and cognitive psychology" (2009, p. x). Her views consider experience and meanings as they occur in the social and cultural worlds of young children and in the context of individual self-organization, which intersect and interact in dynamic cyclical ways.

This book documents the ways in which university student teachers are able to support the learning potential of all children within the context of their home, school, and community. Because of its participatory nature, using narratives written by children, parents, and "teacher scribes," the New Zealand learning story model for assessment in early childhood is used to assess the outcome of this project. Although there are obvious contextual differences between early childhood programs in Southern California and those in New Zealand, there are some important similarities, both in terms of context, regarding collaborators in the education of young children, and in terms of the demands that this emphasis of participatory collaboration creates regarding curriculum.

The New Zealand model of learning story assessment is more comprehensive and more appropriate for participation of teachers, children, and parents, and therefore more authentic. At the same time that university students are beginning their study of curriculum development and working in their student teaching placements, they are also taking a concurrent assessment class along with the curriculum class. The textbook for the assessment class is *Learning Stories: Constructing Learner Identities in Early Education* by Carr and Lee (2012). The professors and students also relied heavily on the New Zealand Ministry of Education website about curriculum development and assessment (New Zealand Ministry of Education, 2010).

Context of Current Study

At our university, in the final year of our early childhood studies undergraduate major, university students concurrently study courses and spend 30 days in county programs working with experienced teachers, staff, and preschool- and primary school–aged children during the fall semester and infants and toddlers in the spring semester. In the university courses, research is presented to build students' knowledge base so that they can continue to synthesize their understanding of children's growth and learning in all domains, community contexts, and the various models of service delivery for programs with young children. Students are supported in this process with an introduction to qualitative research methods for observing, documenting, studying, and analyzing children's learning. The students review theoretical models that have served young children's education around the world and investigate the latest findings in research, which include studies in neuroscience research as related to curriculum creation and assessment. These early childhood majors are required to become experts at observing children's strengths and needs, and then are required to develop their own curriculum plans in collaboration with a particular group of children.

Last, in this ongoing research study, student teachers participate in authentic assessment design through the study and adaptation of the New Zealand learning story model (New Zealand Ministry of Education, 2010). In doing so, they work with early care and education staff and parents from local families, write and implement integrated curricula, practice collaborating with parents to assist with curriculum development, and provide insights from these experiences as they continue their university coursework.

For the purpose of our adaptation of the Learning Story Model, we have labeled our version of this type of assessment *Storying Learning*. We wanted to acknowledge the leadership of the New Zealand colleagues in the field while being transparent about our adaptation of their model. So, to reiterate, at the same time that university students are beginning their study of collaborative (with children) curriculum development and working in their student teaching placements, they are also taking a concurrent assessment class along with the curriculum class. The textbook for the assessment class is *Learning Stories: Constructing Learner Identities in Early Education* by Carr and Lee (2012).

Methods

Three aspects of the overall study are (1) qualitative research methods, (2) integrated curriculum development, and (3) authentic assessment adapted from the Learning Story Model of assessment in New Zealand. From these three features the early childhood teacher education students study, design, implement, and assess curricula based on critical theory. The participation and data collection methods involve participant observation, interviews with families, teacher journals, student teacher research journals, and collections of learners' work samples during their interactions with curricula. The data are analyzed by the categories that emerge, particularly as they relate to the theoretical perspective of critical theory.

The multidisciplinary knowledge base of critical theory affirms the role of criticism and rejects the radical differentiation between theory and practice as two separate poles of a dualism. Critical theory encourages the production and application of theory as a part of the overall search for transformative knowledge. Paulo Freire (1985) popularized critical theory and emphasized participation through personal histories, the sharing of multiple ways of knowing, and transformative action. According to Freire (1997), freedom can only occur when the oppressed reject the image of oppression "and replace it with autonomy and responsibility" (p. 29). Those who adopt Freire's pedagogy need to be aware that it is not made up of techniques to save the world; rather, he feels that "the progressive educator must always be moving out on his or her own, continually reinventing me and reinventing what it means to be democratic in his or her own specific cultural and historical context" (Freire, 1997, p. 308). In other words, a progressive educator must continually strive to reinvent herself/himself and to adapt to the realities of what being democratic means in a particular context. A critical theory framework supports working with migrating families from a variety of historical contexts, language groups, and life experiences. This perspective is supported by data that show that effective learning is a dynamic continuum, always in flux.

Adding to our understanding of critical qualitative research, Kincheloe, McLaren, and Steinberg state:

> It is with our understanding of critical theory and our commitment to critical social research and critical pedagogy that we identify the bricolage as an emancipatory research construct....The French word bricoleur describes a handyman or

handywoman who makes use of the tools available to complete a task (Harper, 1997; Steinberg, 2011). (Kincheloe, McLaren, & Steinberg, 2012, p. 20)

The bricolage is a way to do multidisciplinary research: "[B]ricoleurs move beyond the blinders of particular disciplines and peer through a conceptual window to a new world of research and knowledge production (Denzin, 2003; Kincheloe, McLaren, & Berry, 2004; Steinberg, 2011)" (Kincheloe et al., 2012, p. 21). A researcher as a bricoleur, addresses complexity and employs the use of various research methodologies such as narrative (Janesick, 2010; Park, 2005), hermeneutic interpretation (Jardine, 2006), content analysis (Steinberg, 2011) and others,

Research in this book is framed by critical theory (Freire, 1997) and includes the bricolage as an emancipatory research construct, as described above (Kincheloe et al., 2012). As stated, the French word *bricoleur* describes a handyman or handywoman who uses the tools available to complete a task. Children are capable in this capacity as our co-researchers. Throughout the chapters to come, children taking the research lead as bricoleurs will be introduced. The bricolage creates different ways to read, approach, and use research.

As this research and the resulting implications have revolved around participatory learner-driven curriculum and assessment, I have taken advice from Pinar concerning the interpretation of the developing work. Pinar (2004) advises: "The complicated conversation that is the curriculum requires interdisciplinary intellectuality, erudition, and self-reflexivity. This is not a recipe for high test scores, but a common faith in the possibility of self-realization and democratization, twin projects of social subjective reconstruction"(p. 8).

This ongoing, 5-year qualitative study includes university students from the undergraduate major early childhood studies program, parents and children in various classrooms, university supervisors, teachers, and assistant teachers from county early care and education programs for pre-K to second-grade classrooms and infant and toddler programs. The data collected become massive in amount and detail, and analysis of this type of research can be repetitive. Yet it opens doors for many possibilities of perspectives. As I have written previously (Quintero 2009),

the data of the findings often loops around and intersects in ways that give new insights and make new meanings. Analysis and interpretation worked together to construct meaning. Interpretation pointed to patterns themes and issues in the data and findings were seen in relation to one another and against larger theoretical perspectives, as well as evolving emergent views not found in the "the literature." (p. 8)

Complicated Findings

Findings regarding the collaboration of teacher education students and children to develop creative, responsive curricula will be discussed in Chapters 2 and 3. Then Chapter 4 discusses qualitative examples and selected findings of Storying Learning assessments, which are always connected to curricula being used and modeled after the New Zealand Learning Story methodology. This leads us to revisit and question the access gap, and demands that we consider aspects of what Marian Wright Edelman in the United States and other advocates for young children around the world (Dahlberg et al., 2013) have been saying for years. How can we assume that any curriculum, any assessment design—even by creative, well-educated professionals—can improve programs for young children, until we have considered equity? Many policy makers and educators don't like to talk about the fact that often policy decisions and mandates are based on faulty research. How do we support better attention to children's strengths and needs and support the teachers who work with them to study to be the intellectual experts that children deserve? Chapters 5 and 6 go deeper into these questions and streams of findings that go deeper into issues that connect early childhood programming, politics, policy, and societal contexts and possibilities.

Heckman and others talk a lot about the achievement gap. The achievement gap, the access gap, and the poverty gap are all related. Heckman says,

American students from prosperous backgrounds scored on average 110 points higher on reading tests than disadvantaged students, about the same disparity that exists between the average scores in the United States and Tunisia. It is perhaps the main reason income inequality in the United States is passed down the generations at a much higher rate than in most advanced nations. (Matthews, 2013)

Heckman goes on to say that this suggests "that the angry, worried debate over how to improve the nation's mediocre education—pitting the teachers' unions and the advocates of more money for public schools against the champions of school vouchers and standardized tests—is missing the most important part: infants and toddlers" (Matthews, 2013).

Are these discussions only, or will they lead to policy and funding support? Sadly, to date, not much has changed in terms of policy or funding. Public spending on higher education is more than three times as large as spending on preschool (Isaacs, 2012). A research team found that in 2008, federal and state governments spent somewhat more than $10,000 per child in every year from kindergarten through twelfth grade. By contrast, 3- to 5-year-olds got less than $5,000 for their education and care. Children under 3 got $300 (Isaacs, 2012). But is it all about the money? Our findings and other research suggest that it is not. Chapter 6 goes into more depth on these questions internationally.

Educational programs can build rapport through an informal, nonthreatening environment in which staff members help parents to feel welcomed and comfortable so that they share the important sociocultural meaning in their lives. An integrated curriculum emphasizing family and cultural story and children's literature, especially multicultural children's literature, encourages collaboration and enhances multidirectional participatory learning. In other words, in this context, not only is learning transmitted from teacher to students, but also teachers learn from students, and students from each other. And with this model the curriculum/assessment cycle is meaningful, authentic, and a dynamically connected way to support all learners. We must "search for intelligence where one has previously seen only deficiency" (Kincheloe, 2000, p. 81).

Patterns of findings under the foci of critical, responsive curriculum and authentic assessment for all children have illustrated new questions, provoked new trajectories of informants and connections to dynamic happenings in early childhood internationally. The issues involved in curriculum and assessment point to international discussions about what is "quality" in early care and education and who has the power to decide. These international dynamics highlight the inevitable connections among programs for young children, policies, and politics. Further connections regarding multiple histories, strengths, and needs of young children also illustrate little-discussed refugees and migrating people around the world—and their children who are growing and experiencing life wherever they are living in a variety of situations, with or without support. Chapter 7 explores these complexities. Finally, the complex issues unveiled through our work here of course raise more questions than answers. A school in East London, on a day-to-day, consistent, collaborative basis, concretizes some of the new issues in early childhood colliding with established practice. Strong bricoleur children and supportive, reflective adults help the dynamic program illustrate "what can be" in a unique, inspirational way. They, like the poet Dylan Thomas, know that "One way of ending a story is—."

Notes

1. All names have been changed to protect privacy.
2. British infant schools: Infant schools offer an informal education using child-centered techniques, and have been characterized as progressive, child-centered, open and exploratory.
3. Summerhill School: A co-educational boarding school in Suffolk, England, the original alternative "free" school. It continues to be an influential model for progressive, democratic education around the world.
4. Developmentally Appropriate Practice, often shortened to DAP, is an approach to teaching grounded in the research on how young children develop and learn and in what is known about effective early education. (https://www.naeyc.org/DAP)

References

American Psychological Association. (2002). Guidelines on multicultural education, training, research, practice, and organizational change for psychologists. Retrieved from http://www.apa.org/pi/oema/resources/policy/multicultural-guidelines.aspx

Bloch, M. N. (1992). Critical perspectives on the historical relationship between child development and early childhood education research. In S. Kessler & B. B. Swadener (Eds.), *Reconceptualizing the early childhood curriculum* (pp. 3–20). New York: Teachers College Press.

Bloch, M. N. (2014). Interrogating *Reconceptualizing Early Care and Education* (RECE)—20 years along. In M. N. Bloch, B. B. Swadener, & G. S. Cannella (Eds.), *Reconceptualizing early childhood care and education: A reader* (pp. 19–31). New York: Peter Lang.

Bredekamp, S. (Ed.). (1987). *Developmentally appropriate practice in early childhood programs serving children birth through age 8.* Washington, DC: National Association for the Education of Young Children.

Bredekamp, S., & Copple, C. (Eds.). (1997). *Developmentally appropriate practice in early childhood programs* (rev. ed.). Washington, DC: National Association for the Education of Young Children.

Brown, C., & Lan, Y.-C. (2015). A qualitative metasynthesis of how early educators in international contexts address cultural matters that contrast with developmentally appropriate practice. *Early Education and Development, 26*(1), 22–45.

Cannella, G. S. (1997). *Deconstructing early childhood education: Social justice and revolution.* New York: Peter Lang.

Carr, M., & Lee, W. (2012). *Learning stories: Constructing learner identities in early education.* New York: Sage.

Carr, M., Duncan, J., Lee, W., Jones, C., Marshall, K., & Smith, A. (2009). *Learning in the making: Disposition and design in early education*. Rotterdam, Netherlands: Sense.

Copple, C., & Bredekamp, S. (2009). *Developmentally appropriate practice in early childhood programs serving children from birth through age 8* (3rd ed.). Washington, DC: National Association for the Education of Young Children.

Dahlberg, G., Moss, P. M., & Pence, A. (2013). *Beyond quality in early childhood education and care: Languages of evaluation* (3rd ed.). New York: Routledge.

Denzin, N. K. (2003). *Performance ethnography: Critical pedagogy and the politics of culture*. Thousand Oaks, CA: Sage.

Fox, J., & Rivera-Salgado, G. (Eds.). (2004). *Indigenous Mexican migrants in the United States*. Stanford, CA: Center for Comparative Immigration Studies.

Freire, P. (1985). *The politics of education*. Granby, MA: Bergin & Garvey.

Freire, P. (1997). *Pedagogy of hope*. Granby, MA: Bergin & Garvey.

Grieshaber, S., & Cannella, G. S. (Eds.). (2001). *Embracing identities in early childhood education: Diversity and possibilities*. New York: Teachers College Press.

Harper, D. (1997). *Working knowledge: Skill and community in a small shop*. Chicago: University of Chicago Press.

Heath, S. B. (1983). *Ways with words: Language, life and work in communities and classrooms*. Cambridge, UK: Cambridge University Press.

Iorio, J. M., & Adler, S. M. (2013, March 8). Take a number, stand in line, better yet, be a number, get tracked: The assault of longitudinal data systems on teaching and learning. *Teachers College Record*.

Isaacs, J. B. (2012). *Starting school at a disadvantage: The school readiness of poor children*. Washington, DC: Center on Children and Families, Brookings Institute.

Janesick, V. (2010). *Oral history for the qualitative researcher: Choreographing the story*. New York: Guilford.

Jardine, D. (2006). On hermeneutics: "What happens to us over and above our wanting and doing." In K. Tobin & J. L. Kincheloe (Eds.), *Doing educational research*. (pp. 269–288). Rotterdam, Netherlands: Sense Publishers.

Jones, J. M. (Ed.). (2009). *The psychology of multiculturalism in the schools: A primer for practice, training, and research*. Bethesda, MD: National Association of School Psychologists.

Kincheloe, J. (2000). Certifying the damage: Mainstream educational psychology and the oppression of children. In L. D. Soto (Ed.), *The politics of early childhood education* (pp. 75–84). New York: Peter Lang.

Kincheloe, J., McLaren, P., & Berry, K. (2004). *Rigor and complexity in educational research: Conceptualizing the bricolage*. London: Open University Press.

Kincheloe, J., McLaren, P., & Steinberg, S. R. (2012). Critical pedagogy and qualitative research: Moving to the bricolage. In S. R. Steinberg & G. S. Cannella (Eds.), *Critical qualitative research reader* (pp. 14–32). New York: Peter Lang.

Matthews, D. (2013, February 14). James Heckman: In early childhood education, "Quality really matters." *Washington Post*. Retrieved from http://www.washingtonpost.com/blogs/wonkblog/wp/2013/02/14/james-heckman-in-early-childhood-education-quality-really-matters/

Moll, L. C., Gonzalez, N., & Amanti, C. (2005). *Funds of knowledge: Theorizing practices in households, communities, and classrooms*. Mahwah, NJ: Lawrence Erlbaum Associates.

Nelson, K. (2009). *Young minds in social worlds: Experience, meaning, and memory*. Cambridge, MA: Harvard University Press.

New Zealand Ministry of Education. (2010). ECE Educate [website]. Retrieved from http://www.educate.ece.govt.nz/

O'Laughlin, M. (2009). *The subject of childhood*. New York: Peter Lang.

Park, J. (2005). *Writing at the edge: Narrative and writing process theory*. New York: Peter Lang.

Pinar, W. (2004). *What is curriculum theory?* Mahwah, NJ: Lawrence Erlbaum.

Quintero, E. P. (2009). *Critical literacy in early childhood education: Artful story and the integrated curriculum*. New York: Peter Lang.

Quintero, E. P. (2010). Something to say: Children learning through story. *Early Education and Development, 21*(3), 372–391.

Quintero, E. P. (2012). Early childhood collaborations: Learning from migrant families and children. In R. W. Blake & B. E. Blake (Eds.), *Becoming a teacher: Using narrative as reflective practice. A cross-disciplinary approach* (pp. 168–189). New York: Peter Lang.

Quintero, E. P. (2014). Juan, Melina, and friends: Guides for reconceptualizing readiness. In W. Parnell & J. M. Iorio (Eds.), *Reconceptualizing readiness in early childhood education* (pp. 179–190). New York: Springer.

Quintero, E., & Velarde, M. C. (1990). Intergenerational Literacy: A developmental, bilingual approach. *Young Children, 45*(4), 10–15.

Schweinhart, L. J., Barnes, H. V., Weikart, D. P., Barnett, W. S., & Epstein, A. S. (1993). *Significant benefits: The High/Scope Perry Preschool Study through age 27*. Ypsilanti, MI: High/Scope Press.

Steinberg, S. (2011). Critical cultural studies research: Bricolage in action. In K. Tobin & J. Kincheloe (Eds.), *Doing educational research* (2nd ed.) (pp. 87–116). Rotterdam, Netherlands: Sense Publishing.

Steinberg, S., & Kincheloe, J. (2009). Smoke and mirrors: More than one way to be diverse and multicultural. In S. Steinberg (Ed.), *Diversity and multiculturalism: A reader* (pp. 3–22). New York: Peter Lang.

Swadener, E. B., & Lubeck, S. (Eds.). (1995). *Children and families "at promise": Deconstructing the discourse of risk*. Albany: SUNY Press.

Wright, A. (2005). *The death of Ramón González*. Austin: University of Texas Press.

Yoshikawa, H., Weiland, C., Brooks-Gunn, J., Burchinal, M. R., Espinosa, L. M., Gormley, W. T., ... Zaslow, M. J. (2013). Investing in our future: The evidence base on preschool education. Ann Arbor, MI: Society for Research in Child Development. Retrieved from http://www.srcd.org/policy-media/policy-updates/meetings-briefings/investing-our-future-evidence-base-preschool

· 2 ·

CURRICULUM IN EARLY CHILDHOOD: A COMPLICATED CONVERSATION AMONG UNIVERSITY TEACHER EDUCATION STUDENTS

What is curriculum, and where does it come from, and who decides what will be learned? Since times of prehistory, this has been an important question (Campbell, 2008; Eisler, 1988). Going again to several recent studies that connect experiences with people and environments to learning and potential, it is obvious that in terms of young children, curriculum is everything.

Bloch (2014) reflects:

> [W]hose voices and knowledge count? Whose values are embedded in what we think is appropriate curriculum and for whom? Critical questions and some responses are illustrated...in the critically significant work of the Maori/non-Maori researchers' participation in the development and continued critique of the *Te Whāriki* early childhood curriculum (originally published in 1997); Ritchie & Rau, 2007, 2009).... The mental research (Pacini-Ketchabaw, 2010; Taylor, 2013) that has allowed for the imagining of the "natures" of child with/in his/their ecological and cultural context has added powerful dimensions to possibilities for curriculum theory and pedagogy. (p. 24)

And returning to Yoshikawa et al. (2013) and many others, the claims made are extensive:

Early experiences in the home, in other care settings, and in communities interact with genes to shape the developing nature and quality of the brain's architecture. The growth and then environmentally based pruning of neuronal systems in the first years support a range of early skills, including cognitive (early language, literacy, math), social (theory of mind, empathy, prosocial), persistence, attention, and self-regulation and executive function skills (the voluntary control of attention and behavior). Later skills—in schooling and employment—build cumulatively upon these early skills. (Yoshikawa et al., 2013, p. 3)

And, to look forward to Chapter 5, Penn (2014) offers criticism of broad claims about neuroscience research and young children's learning that often has little documentation in the literature. However, regardless of our current varying perspectives, it seems to those of us who take our observations of, and thinking about, children seriously, curriculum is everything in a child's life. It is the whole integrated picture, and it begins with our earliest memories.

Another Way to Create and Implement Early Childhood Curricula

This study about early learning, and this book, point to the holistic weaving of context, culture, affect, and cognition, and the necessity for learners of all ages to be the masters of their own learning journeys. This premise illustrates the three tenets of critical theory: participatory responsibility, multiple sources of knowledge, and transformative action. I work with groups of student teachers in urban and rural schools. We support students' multiple languages and recognize ways that multiple knowledge sources, identities, and language forms can contribute to the formation of new relationships and meanings. As a community of scholars in a wide variety of classrooms, we respect the children's backgrounds, plan carefully for their current experiences in school, and prepare them for future challenges, including competitive learning programs, standardized testing, and a variety of future journeys.

As a basis for integrated curriculum, as stated in Chapter 1, critical theory guides our work in this study and in early care and education because it emphasizes participation through personal histories, sharing of multiple ways of knowing, and transformative action. Critical literacy, an aspect of critical theory, addresses issues in an integrated and participatory way. We define critical literacy as a process of constructing and critically using language (oral and written) as a means of expression, interpretation, and/or transformation of our lives and the lives of those around us. The teacher education students document their journeys as they experience the method in their teacher education classes and as they use the method with young children. They practice using this critical framework for focusing on story, multicultural children's literature, and creating literacy opportunities that extend beyond the classroom to use the words of their families and communities for literacy education. Chapter 3 will go into depth, illustrating teacher education students using this model with children.

Early childhood studies students participating in this qualitative study begin thinking about integrated curriculum by thinking of their own family histories. What was meaningful in their interactions with loved ones and other people? What were examples of the beginnings of understanding story and communication? One teacher education student, examining her personal stories related to her integrated learning as a young child, wrote in a journal entry:

> I remember that my family had a lot of books, but not children's books. My grandfather and I had very good relationship and in fact, we are still very close. When I was young, we used to live together as a big family. It was always the nighttime, when I was going to bed, he told me the folktales. He didn't have a book. It was a real folktale that he knew from a long time ago. Those stories were amazing. I imagined all the characters, and I imagined all the happenings that came out of my grandfather's mouth. While I was thinking about the story, I fell into sleep and dreamed about it.
>
> On the other hand, my grandmother used to tell me her real-life stories. For her, it was real, but for me, it was a tale. She lived in a completely different society from mine. She talked about how her house, school, family, marriage, the Korean war… etc. It was all about her. However, it was also a culture and history lesson for me.
>
> Every night, I begged for a story from them. Oftentimes they said, "I already told you about that story, didn't I?" I replied, "Yes, but that's okay, I can listen one more time.…" I still remember every single story and moment that we shared. (Quintero, 2009a, p. 83)

The teachers in an earlier study talked about the importance of the passing on of stories by parents and grandparents. They felt that this was an important legacy passed down through the generations. One teacher reported that her West Indian grandmother passed on teachings through folk tales. Another teacher talked about both his grandfather and grandmother, and noted that passing on history through stories in his American Indian family during his youth was done orally. They gathered around a campfire, and the elders would talk and tell stories (Rummel & Quintero, 1997).

Family Histories and Curriculum Development

The teacher education students address what integrated curriculum might mean for learning and for meaningful practice both inside and outside the classroom. For example, in Ms. Rafiq's first-grade class, every child came to this country from another country, recently. Some never spoke English before kindergarten last year. Some speak the English of Guyana and don't qualify for English-language services, but the dialect is so different that it is as if the children are working with a second language. Some children are from Central America, some are from India, some are from Russia, and others are from Haiti. And they become engaged participants in the poetry that Ms. Rafiq adores and introduces them to.

She began her collaborations in qualitative action research with her first graders by sharing with them part of a poem she had written as a part of a "Where I'm From" list poem activity in her university class. Her belief is that teaching and learning involves sharing and disclosing personal stories as a collaboration to learn others' stories and encourage critical literacy. Ms. Rafiq's poem includes the following stanza:

> I am from spices and scarves,
> hand-me-downs and baseball cards
> I am from friendly neighbors and bus stops
> and a place where we walk and not drive
> I am from Ahmed and Razia
> who came here to give me a better life. (Quintero, 2009b, p. 7)

With this beginning, she shares her family stories and involves her students in writing their own poetry through her literacy program. They also make dioramas for a social studies project. The dioramas are set in the countries from which their families come, and after a mini-lesson on voice as a part of the week's Writers Workshop, the children plan what the characters in the dioramas are talking about in their own voices. They write the words, sometimes in English, sometimes in the home languages of the families.

Participating students dwell on a deep understanding of the assumption that words, deeds, policy, practice, and theory application are inseparably linked in our world and this work. We cannot pretend that education is neutral, nor can the practice be done in isolation. With this perspective, family and community become a context for studying integrated curriculum. Going back to Chapter 1, and information from Carr et al. (2009) and Moll et al.

(2005) about the importance of lived experiences enriching integrated curriculum, the stories of the teacher education students and the children concretize the advice of the researchers. The research stresses that implementation of integrated curricula across child experiential and cultural domains (for example, socio-emotional development as it connects with cognitive conceptual development in language and math) supports feasible, integrated learning (Nelson, 2009).

Furthermore, in our work we hold as nonnegotiable that curriculum be integrated and experientially, culturally, and linguistically responsive. Thus, it is important to consider the children mentioned above in Ms. Rafiq's first-grade class. Her context is a largely immigrant neighborhood in Queens in New York City, and thus it has a large proportion of children from around the world. This is representation of the context, true, and at the same time it is representative and indicative of demographic changes around the world.

Family Histories and Theoretical Foundations

Consequently, in the discussion about curriculum for whom, we also must revisit work compiled by Brown and Lan (2014) that analyzes the cultural clashes between *Developmentally Appropriate Practice*[1] and cultural, family, and historical values in programs for young children and families around the world. They report that in one study, Lee and Tseng (2008) questioned *Developmentally Appropriate Practice in Early Childhood Programs* (Bredekamp & Copple, 1997) and felt that enough had not been done to work past the universal assumptions (regarding child development) found in this work. They noted that while the 1997 revised version of *Developmentally Appropriate Practice* recognized social and cultural differences among children, and acknowledged the multiplicity of different individual characteristics and lived experiences, there remained generalizations about universal human development and learning. Lee and Tseng (2008) warn, "The multiplicities and differences are not acknowledged but instead are dangerously ignored while assumptions are made about a singular norm and homogenous universal standard" (p. 184). Lee and Tseng say that DAP "not only confirms certain social privileges and cultural norms, but also pathologizes those who are already socially disadvantaged or culturally different" (p. 194), which mirrors many previously mentioned critiques of this document (e.g., Polakow, 1989).

These critical questions point us to the work of Katherine Nelson (2009), whose views consider experience and meanings as they occur in the social and cultural worlds of young children and in the context of individual self-organization, which intersect and interact in dynamic cyclical ways. Dahlberg, Moss, and Pence (2013) note that as early as 1988, Gregory Bateson warned that we live with the illusion that the map (of child developmental norms) is the territory, or the landscape, and the name is the same as the named. Dahlberg et al. (2013) go on to explain:

> Not only do these abstract maps drawn from theories of child development make us lose sight of what is really taking place in the everyday lives of children and peda-gogues, since reality is more complex, contextualized and perspectival than the maps we draw, the descriptions we make and the categories we use…but they can easily objectify children and ourselves as pedagogues and researchers. The child becomes an object of normalization, via the child-centered pedagogy that has grown out from developmental psychology, with developmental assessments acting as a technology of normalization determining how children should be. In the process power enters through the creation of a type of hierarchy among children according to whether or not they have reached a specific state, and achieving the norm and preventing or correcting deviations for the norm take over the pedagogical practice. (p. 39)

Children are the consummate communicators about the personal, and communal experiences they bring to early education must be included and built upon. Children weave their webs of connection to others in their families, communities, and the world. They don't live or grow in a bubble, and they don't sit in school and "study" to be adults, with their attention only on what "will be" when they are adults. They are experts at being "in the moment." All children, from all backgrounds and histories, learn through their stories while engaging in play and other daily activities. They experience development in multiple domains and engage in multidimensional learning when given opportunity and encouragement.

As stated in Chapter 1, this work around integrated curriculum design and implementation in early learning points to the holistic weaving of context, culture, affect, and cognition, and the necessity for learners of all ages to be the masters of their own learning journeys. Our work uses integrated curriculum that includes all the traditional content areas of study, the arts, and new forms of cross-disciplinary ways of knowing. By using a critical literacy approach with multicultural children's literature and the words of many community members who are not currently "heard," this environment of possibility is optimized for students.

Curriculum by and for Whom?

As the work continues throughout the semesters in the university classes, and as findings emerge, theoretical and current research relating to the categories of findings is addressed. Of course, many of the foundational assumptions, early childhood methods, and overlapping issues relate to current research in the United States regarding quality indicators for early childhood programming for younger learners. It is our contention that quality indicators cannot be identified without an analysis of context and cultural beliefs and realities about young children's experiences. And relatedly, the discussion about "curriculum for whom" must include an acknowledgement of "curriculum *by* whom"?

Large well-known corporations and private foundations have sponsored much of the research. These named curricula are almost entirely prepackaged, expensive curriculum plans offered by publishing corporations. The implicit message from their marketing and from their funders who don't understand the intricacies of curriculum for young children, furthermore, is that the only curricula that are research-based are those that are "named," or published by well-known and well-funded companies. A further unspoken implication is that if programs that use these "named" curricula are representative of "quality," then programs that use teacher/participant-developed curricula are not research-based, and therefore, not quality.

This is a dangerous perpetuation of the notion that teachers are not capable of designing and implementing curricula; they are mere technicians, not intellectuals (Giroux, 1988). From my many years of working with early childhood teacher education in community college programs, university bachelor's programs, and graduate programs, I can say unequivocally that all teachers in early care and education who have studied and completed a teacher education program do create curricula that are research-based. And without question, participants who happen to be children, or multilingual, or from cultural histories from around the world, can be counted on to contribute richly to curriculum design.

Furthermore, teaching to the "curriculum guide" that is not created by teachers actually working with children is not effective. It takes away the opportunities for teachers to use their knowledge and dispositions to design a curriculum, or at the very least, to adapt a published curriculum to build upon the strengths of families in the form of rich family history, multiple languages, and a variety of life experiences. And it prevents early care and education professionals from building on inspirational moments that can potentially be a part of every day.

Participants and Collaborators

Again, the research here is a qualitative study that documents early childhood studies teacher education students' work as they journey through their own teacher development process in literacy and curriculum development. The participants are teachers, student teachers, and their pupils (pre-K through grade 3, including children with special needs and dual-language learners). The participants are students in the final year of a bachelor's degree program, master's degree/credential students, and practicing teachers studying to enhance their learning in early childhood studies. All participants are actively involved in working with children in either a student teaching or teaching situation. Some programs are in urban schools, some in rural schools, and most programs (82%) serve families in poverty. In almost every program (96%) children who are dual-language learners participate. In the university classes, the early childhood studies student participants study a developmental-systems approach (Nelson, 2009), critical theory, constructivist theories, and critical race theory in addition to other foundational theories relating to early care and education.

In the early childhood studies curriculum classes beginning in their senior year of undergraduate study, students have qualitative narrative assignments such as: (a) writing narrative descriptions (from journals) of children's development, strengths, and needs, and the context of the classroom; (b) writing brief accounts of children interacting in school using their home languages (other than English and including English), addressing the following questions: What do the children say? When do they use their home language? What supports their doing this? (the adults, the children, the materials, the personality of the child?); and (c) noticing details about children's literacy and mathematics knowledge (at the placement), answering the following questions: What do you see as the children's strengths? What do they know? How do you know they know this?

Additionally, the teacher education students participate in in-class activities involving reviewing current research and discussing multicultural literature in order to become more adept at recognizing and documenting strengths, funds of knowledge, and the needs of families and communities.

They learn to listen to families. In addition to doing class work related to collecting data about children and cultural contexts, students are assigned to conduct ethnographic interviews with parents of some of the children in their student-teaching classrooms.

The methods used to collect data and document the learning are participant observation, interviews, teacher journals, and collection of learners' work samples. The data are analyzed by categories that emerge, particularly as they relate to the theoretical perspectives of critical theory (Freire, 1973, 1997; Kincheloe & Steinberg, 1998). As we struggle to present findings about children and narrative, which we believe embodies meaningful learning of the deepest sort, we have taken advice from Pinar (2004):

> The complicated conversation that is the curriculum requires interdisciplinary intellectuality, erudition, and self-reflexivity. This is not a recipe for high test scores, but a common faith in the possibility of self-realization and democratization, twin projects of social subjective reconstruction. (p. 8)

Pinar's label of "complicated conversations" frames the discussion of our university classes and later, the patterns of interrelated themes of the findings. The findings show that integrated curriculum through personal story through play, children's connections through literature, and children's use of narrative in writing all the while encourage all areas of integrated curriculum study in experientially and culturally appropriate experiences.

These complicated conversations in the qualitative study come from participants' discussions of research in the field, from the wisdom of informants through their interviews, and from the observations during the study. In addition to the complicated conversations, excerpts from our university classes setting up the construct of creating critical, integrated curriculum for the early childhood studies students are included. The university students illustrate not only the themes as they emerged in the early childhood classrooms, but also the aspects of critical theory—participant histories, multiple forms of knowledge, and transformative action. Following this, in Chapter 3, we present excerpts from case studies of the university students working with children using this model. These case study excerpts show some of the interactions in various classrooms when this creation of integrated curriculum based on critical literacy was implemented.

Reiterating the use of the construct of bricoleur (Kincheloe, McLaren, & Steinberg, 2012), we employ multiple perspectives as we consider curricula and theoretical constructs that inform curricula. We stress that we, as professionals and students who study, work with, and learn from children, are bricoleurs. Again, the French word *bricoleur* describes a handyman or handywoman who uses the tools available to complete a task. This research construct (Kincheloe et al., 2012) is emancipatory, fraught with opportunity and challenge. Children are capable in this capacity as our co-researchers and co-creators of curriculum. Children aren't scientists; they are children being experts in the moment and making connections with others. Through the narrative art of stories, children give meaning to our lives (Andrews, Squire, & Tamboukou, 2008). They can lead and teach us if we listen.

As early childhood professionals with research frames in our repertoire that historically were informed by a range of Western foci from Vygotsky, Piaget, Bronfenbrenner, Montessori, to Malaguzzi, we begin with critical theory as a frame for research and practice in this complicated world of learners with multiple strengths, multiple histories, and multiple needs. By studying children from other perspectives in addition to the Western "lens" that is still prevalent in many academic circles and texts, we have worked at moving beyond more traditional child development approaches by studying critical theory (Freire, 1984; Kincheloe, 2000) and critical race theory (Ladson-Billings, 2005). In addition, we have been encouraged by the work of Lee (2008) and Spencer (2006) that takes systems theory beyond the middle-class, Western-focused emphasis to understand a broader view of development. Scholarly work by Lee (2008) in the areas of cognitive research and cultural research has influenced the analysis of our research. As Lee (2008) points out, "The cognitively oriented studies of how people learn are not in dialogue with those that focus on culture and cognition (Bransford, Brown, & Cocking, 1999); the multiculturalists are not in dialogue with the culture and cognition researchers (Banks & Banks, 1995); cognitively oriented research and the world of human development have little to do with each other" (p. 268). Although there clearly are differences among these paradigms, they share a number of fundamental propositions:

(1) Context matters—contexts help to shape people, and people shape contexts,

(2) Routine practices count, and

(3) The cognitive, social, physical, and biological dimensions of both individuals and contexts interact in important ways. (Lee, 2008, p. 268)

Finally, we emphasize the recent work of Katherine Nelson (2009), whose research outlines a developmental-systems approach where "Meaning belongs first to persons, and personal meaning filters cultural offerings. Thus the symbiosis grows in developmental time, at least partially through the openness accorded to culture by the child's own mind" (p. 267).

Focusing on integrated curriculum and children's engagement with story as a framework for integrated curriculum, just to quickly preview our findings, in compatibility with critical theory and the emphasis on family history, we found three areas that illustrated the importance of personal and community story. We see story as a way for young learners to experience many integrated content learning opportunities and social/emotional learning opportunities in meaningful ways. Children's pretend and symbolic play is a way we see story supporting children's meaningful learning. Interaction with children's literature is another way stories become a frame for an integrated curriculum. And children's writing about their own ideas in narrative form is a way to generate meaningful integrated learning. We see integrated curriculum as it reflects the social, emotional, and cognitive domains of young children in the context of their communities and historical richness. This leads to an authentic way to address experiences with core content standards as a part of teachers using narrative in play and personal story, with children's literature, and by using child-created books to cross boundaries and interact with different constructs within their world of learning. In turn, in each of the categories of findings, the three tenets of critical theory are apparent in the early childhood context. These three tenets are (1) participation through personal story, culture, history, and language, (2) multiple sources of knowledge, and (3) transformative action.

Context of Early Childhood Studies Majors

At our university, in the final year of our early childhood studies major, university students concurrently study in courses and spend 30 days in county programs working with experienced teachers, staff, and preschool- and primary school–aged children during the fall semester and infants and toddlers in the spring semester. In the university courses, information and research are presented to students so that they can continue to synthesize their understanding of children's experiences, community contexts, and the various models of programs for young children. Students are supported in this process by the use of qualitative methods for observing and documenting children's learning. The students review theoretical models that have addressed young children's education around the world, and investigate the latest research regarding children's growth, interests, and potential as related to curriculum development and assessment. These early childhood majors are required to become experts at observing children's strengths and needs, and then are required to develop their own integrated curriculum plans for working with a particular group of children. Lastly, in this ongoing research study, student teachers participate in authentic assessment design through the study and adaptation of the New Zealand Learning Story Model (New Zealand Ministry of Education, 2015). In doing all this, they work with early-care and education staff and parents from local families, write and implement integrated curricula, and provide insights from these experiences as they continue their university course work.

This research documents the ways in which university student teachers are able to support the learning potential of all children within the context of their homes, school, and community. Because of its participatory nature, using narratives written by children, parents, and "teacher scribes," the New Zealand Learning Story Model for assessment in early childhood is used to assess the outcome of this project. Although there are obvious contextual differences between early childhood programs in Southern California and those in New Zealand, there are some important similarities, both in terms of context, regarding collaborators in the education of young children, and in terms of the demands that this emphasis of participatory collaboration creates regarding curriculum development and assessment.

Throughout the course work, the students in the university class use qualitative research methods, design responsive integrated curriculum, and create authentic assessments. The participation and data collection methods involve participant observation, interviews with families, teacher journals, and collections of learners' work samples during their interaction with curricula. The data are analyzed by the categories that emerge, particularly as they relate to the theoretical perspective of critical theory.

What the Work Looks Like

The teacher education students participate in a variety of activities based on critical theory in teacher education courses before they begin planning, collaborating with children and teachers, and implementing similar activities for the children they work with. They begin writing their autobiographical narratives and doing their qualitative research (Ely, Anzul, Friedman, Garner, & McCormack-Steinmetz, 1991) at the outset of their participation, and continue throughout their program of study with the use of critical literacy in their own learning as adults, and then with young learners in the classrooms they participate in. The case study excerpts from participating student teachers that opened this chapter illustrate ways they connect their own personal histories to the work surrounding the creation of integrated curriculum.

Learning to Listen and Document

In curriculum classes beginning their senior year of undergraduate study, students are given qualitative narrative assignments about learning to observe and listen to children, such as: (a) writing a narrative description (from journals) of children's participation, strengths, and needs and the context of the classroom; (b) writing a brief account of children in school using their home language (other than English), and addressing the following questions: "What do the children say?" "When do they use their home language?" "What supports their doing this? (the adults, the children, the materials, the personality of the child?)"; and (c) noticing details about children's literacy and mathematics knowledge (at the placement), and answering the following questions: "What do you see as the children's strengths?" "What do they know?" "How do you know they know this?" Right about here is where we have much strong discussion about the absolute necessity for all curriculum development to stem from children's interests, histories (including languages), strengths, and needs. We discuss what that means, what it might look like, and ways we may all become more effective listeners and ethnographers.

Student teachers then begin developing integrated content-learning experiences for children, focusing on the history and culture of the children's families. It is important that the student teachers "tune in" to the children and their families and build upon their strengths, never minimizing their responsibility to provide opportunities for teaching strong academic foundations for future educational success. Based on one assignment, a student teacher working with 4-year-olds wrote in her reflective journal:

> One concept that the children are exploring in the classroom is the concept of light via an overhead projector that projects onto the ceiling. There are several children pushing colored jewels and a stencil onto the projector. They push them around and

are experimenting with how the objects appear on the ceiling when moved. Nearby, there are children indirectly associated with this activity. One child is drawing on a whiteboard the images she sees on the ceiling. The child next to her is engaged in the same task. She says, "La mariposa está muerta (The butterfly is dead)." She continues drawing the image.

I think this demonstrates critical literacy because the children are using different mediums of understanding to demonstrate the concept of storytelling through their work. While one child is using objects to tell their story on the overhead, another child is transforming this activity to tell their story via images.

I saw a teacher supporting children's literacy by sharing an exciting story with them at circle time. The teacher uses storytelling techniques, which draws the children in. She asks questions to spark curiosity. They seem very interested. The teacher lets the children know that the book is available in the library. She encourages children to visit the library to read books during free time.

The next time I visit there are children in the library. The teacher tells me later that she was concerned because the children never visited that area of the classroom and wants to encourage the children to explore books with their friends and independently. (Quintero, 2009a, p. 24)

Another student wrote:

Recently I observed a child with special needs developing critical literacy in her personalized way. She is 3 years old and naptime is the most difficult time of day for her. She is rarely able to take a nap, and has never taken a nap during naptime at her program. On goods days she can lie quietly for most of the time, but it is a constant struggle for both the child and the teacher. Her most successful coping mechanism is reading a book. She only has very basic literacy skills, such as naming letters and the corresponding sounds. However, this child will flip through each and every page and tell herself a reasonably complex story that is consistent with the pictures in the book. When she is finished with one book, she will begin with the next book.

I would give her age-appropriate books to read and allowed her to spend any amount of time with one book until she was ready for another book. Though naptime is a quiet time for the children, I encouraged her to whisper to herself at a reasonable volume. It seemed essential.

The child is not only using her imagination to create a storyline, but she is also learning a useful coping mechanism in order to be quiet while others are sleeping. By practicing coping skills, she is developing her intrapersonal intelligence and is learning how to assert her control in a positive manner. During a good day, when naptime ends her increased confidence in her abilities is obvious. (Quintero, 2009a, p. 19)

The following brief excerpt from a series of university class lessons illustrates the importance of focusing on the content as well as the process in curriculum development and learning. The university class studies research that documents teaching with critical literacy using problem-posing that focuses on children's lived experiences and children's literature. This method nourishes an integrated curriculum that supports young children's meaningful learning (Quintero, 2009a; Quintero & Rummel, 2003). Simply defined, the problem-posing method is comprised of several components. These are: *listening*, *dialogue*, and *action*. In this method, participants:

- listen to their own histories through reflective writing and sharing of participants' stories, and gather new information in the form of mini-lectures, expert presentations, or scholarly research and academic information;
- dialogue about information that was shared and presented during the listening activities; discuss issues of power that have shaped their identities and current families, schools, and communities contexts; and make connections to the situations of the children and families they work with using personal and historical information;
- collaborate on various curricular activities that encourage and support action or transformation on the part of children, families, and educators.

The adult student teachers practice in the university class and brainstorm with peers and instructors about ways problem-posing might be used with young children.

Listening to Our Own Family Stories

The early childhood studies students participating in this qualitative study begin their integrated curriculum class by thinking of their own family histories. What was meaningful in their interactions with loved ones and other people? How do these memories connect with their own evolving beliefs about how young children learn?

A teacher education student wrote about her family history and the dynamics of learning:

> A memory I have of my mother with literacy is singing and dancing while doing chores. I remember her dancing around with a broom and whistling. She taught me how to whistle and hum to music. My mother did not read or write but she would always sit down with us to do our homework. She would also buy the newspaper and read it. Little did I know that all she did was look at pictures and cut the coupons. Now I understand a lot of things that happened when I was younger and appreciate my mother more. (Quintero, 2009a, p. 95)

The mother mentioned here nurtured a family tradition that involved imagination and pretend story. This is told by the same student teacher, and the young boy with the magic book is the grandson of the mother mentioned above.

> In my family we have a "magic book." The magic book got its name because everyone in my family tells a different story every time it's told. Our family members have different types and levels of education and life experiences. My nephew was given this magic book when he was a few weeks old. It is a wordless storybook, and my sister made it a habit to read to him this "magic book" every night. As he got older he would carry his book around and ask different family members to read him this wordless book. We explained to him that anyone could use imagination and make up a new story every time. The reasons we started this tradition was because children tend to memorize a story, and when someone else reads the story a different way, not as they know it, the child corrects the adult. My nephew is 6 years old now and he has a 1-year-old sister. He continues the tradition with his younger cousins and his sister. The rest of the family also continues the tradition, but now my nephew likes to read them the "magic book" himself. It's amazing to me that he never repeats the story; it's always different. What I find more interesting is that he individualizes the story according to whomever he reads the story to, someone different. (Quintero, 2009a, p. 111)

In a subsequent class, after watching a short video clip of an interview with Sandra Cisneros in which she discusses her revelation when she entered graduate school. She explained that her own history, language, and set of cultural experiences in Chicago were never included in the narratives she studied in school—ever. These personal narratives became the basis of her writing for *The House on Mango Street* (1991).

In the dialogue section, students are asked to discuss with a partner their chosen memories of their family literacy history. Following the discussion, information is distributed related to the history, language, and culture of the

Mixtec people (the indigenous community comprising many of the agricultural workers in our county). Students then work in small groups to consider ways to incorporate some of the information into the curriculum activities that they are planning.

The class agenda for a related class session followed the following format:

1. *Listening:* The students listened to author Sandra Cisneros reflect on the issue of connecting personal family history to writing.
2. *Dialogue:* The students shared aspects of their memories of their family literacy history with a partner, and discussed ways that their thinking about these experiences related to the issues Cisneros discussed.
3. *Action:* The teacher distributed information related to the history, language, and culture of the Mixtec people, and in small groups students worked on using some of the new information as a part of their lesson development for young children.

Soon after this series, the listening aspect of the class, for example, might begin with a mini-lecture reviewing curriculum theory and reiterating the connections of this work to early childhood foundational theories and models. Then, teacher education students might be asked to journal about their personal research framework for early childhood education. They first would reflect on their own experiences with emerging literacy development in their own lives.

Connected to theories of foundational models and theories of curriculum, the instructor noted the complexity of curriculum standards, stressing that some curriculum standards are the result of work by early childhood professional organizations, and other standards are developed by state and federal groups and mandated for various age groups and grade levels. In this discussion, the levels were:

1. *Listening:* The instructor gave a mini-lecture about curriculum standards in general and early childhood education in particular. Critical perspectives, family histories, family hopes and dreams, and the responsibilities of the bricolage were explained.
2. *Dialogue:* The instructor asked the university students to discuss with a partner the connections they saw between professional curriculum standards and their own views of curriculum (philosophical and theoretical frame). The instructions were given as follows: "Please discuss

in small groups ways that you see your own philosophies and views of curriculum relate to, are similar to, or are different from some of the 'model standards' that were shared in the mini-lecture."

3. *Action:* Students investigated the websites of professional organizations and government departments of education to view a variety of examples of standards and guidelines for integrated curriculum development. The Web search was followed by another dialogue activity in which students were asked to discuss the ways in which their research frames influence their choices for curriculum development. For action homework, the university students were asked to write a detailed narrative describing the context of the program in which they were student teaching, including information about the community of the families, the philosophy of the program, the environment of the classroom, and details about a few of the children's strengths and needs. When the university students brought their narratives back to class and discussed them, they were asked to reflect on and write about whether standards and curriculum guidelines enhance our work to support all families and children or inhibit this work.

Listening to Multicultural Children's Literature

In addition to studying and problematizing curriculum standards and guidelines, critical literacy, issues of access, and family strengths and needs, the university classes allocate an hour or more each week for students to participate in activities that use children's literature as a focal point to integrate other content areas such as math and science into curriculum design. For example, the focus may be on problem-posing with math and storybooks. A variety of storybooks appropriate for 4- to 8-year-olds was distributed to each table of four university students. The task was for the four students at each table to choose a storybook and agree on an age group of children for whom they would create a problem-posing lesson that integrates literacy, math, and at least one other content area.

For the listening section, each group appointed a reader to read aloud the book their group had chosen. For the dialogue section, they were asked to discuss the story in their groups and plan a problem-posing lesson (instructional sequence) related to it for their target age group. The group then made connections and/or suggestions based on Smith (2012) and were asked to include aspects in their activity that relate to literacy and at least one additional content area. For the action section, the groups charted their problem-posing/instructional sequence on white paper to display. As they shared their planning with the class, the groups were asked to lead discussions about other activities that would give children opportunities to develop this math concept in their classes, paying attention to maintaining opportunities for the children to make choices in their learning. They were encouraged to explore possible connections to children's culture, home language, and daily experiences.

Listening to Dual-Language Learners

Another brief excerpt from a university class session relating to our strong commitment to dual-language learners shows the integrated format used somewhat differently.

In the opening activity for the listening section, students are asked to review their personal field notes for information about children's use of their home languages (other than English) in school, and to answer the following questions: "What do they say?" "When do they use their home language?" and "What supports their doing this (the adults, the children, the materials, the personality of the child)?"

In the dialogue section, students are asked to discuss what they had noted about children's use of their home languages, and explain that in detail to their small groups. Then, for the action section, they are asked to analyze the following questions about their observations in their journals: "Is this critical literacy?" and "In what ways does this relate to your research frameworks?"

Then the class continues with another listening section. The instructor reads the storybook *I Love Saturdays y Domingos* by Alma Flor Ada (2002), which tells the story of a girl's life with both her English-speaking and her Spanish-speaking grandparents. For the dialogue section, students are asked to relate the story to issues discussed that night in class. They then go back to another listening section, listening to *Friends from the Other Side/Amigos del otro lado* by Gloria Anzaldúa (1997), which is a story about a young girl befriending a boy who had recently moved to an American neighborhood from Mexico with his mother, without documentation. The story involves issues of friendship, coping with bullying, experiences related to how political situations in communities affect children, and cultural traditions including sharing food and natural healing.

For the dialogue section, the students participate in a large group discussion that addresses the topics surrounding appropriate ways to address controversial issues and teachers' responsibilities to do so. For the action section, students read and share some teacher research articles addressing controversial issues from the journal *Rethinking Schools Online*. Then, in groups, they are asked to plan centers that could be set up to go with the themes addressed in story.

Context Influencing Aspects of Methodology

Recently in the state of California there has been legislation to mandate the creation of transitional kindergarten to provide responsive educational opportunities for children whose birthdays mean they are very young, and not always developmentally able (again, are the right questions being asked about the situation young children find themselves in?), to participate in traditional kindergarten. As Bloch (2014) notes, this is clearly a situation in which we must push for changes and "ruptures" in language, policy, and practice. To be bluntly honest, and to oversimplify what happened, legislation was passed instituting a mandate to implement a certain number of transitional kindergarten programs as pilot programs. Because the state did not have time to develop, hold public hearings, and run trials on new standards for curriculum implementation in transitional kindergarten, transitional kindergarten teachers were directed to use as the standards for curriculum development an alignment of the *California Preschool Learning Foundations* (California Department of Education, 2014) and the *California State Common Core Standards* (California Department of Education, 2012).

In other words, alignment documents were provided by state education professionals and suggestions were made, but teachers were actually able to create their own curriculum based upon their professional knowledge and experience and the strengths and needs of the particular populations of children they work with. It is ironic that in 2014, the idea that teachers creating their own curricula is an unusual and exciting event.

For example, the *California Preschool Learning Foundations* guides us to include in our curriculum for young children the developmental domains of social/emotional development, cognitive development, and physical development. Additionally, the guidelines include emphasis on language and literacy, English language development, mathematics, visual and performing arts, health, history/social science, and science.

The *California Common Core Standards* for kindergarten include: English language arts and literacy in history and social studies; science and technical studies concepts about print; writing strategies; and mathematics, number sense, classification and patterning, measurement, geometry, and mathematical reasoning.

So, even if teachers don't philosophically believe in the idea of including all children's interests, strengths, and needs in curriculum planning, we must learn to do an integration of all of this to be able to meet the standards required by most states. And, in all honesty, I hope and believe that by participating in this work teachers who aren't enthusiastic about this method will be won over by the children bricoleurs—they are excellent at integrating content based on their interests. This pragmatic approach also supports teacher education students in the early childhood studies university programs that prepare professionals to work with children from birth to age 8. So, to come back to Dylan Thomas, as we did at the end of Chapter 1, "One way of ending a story is—," and there are many types and versions of the "one way." This is what we promote and encourage the risk taking to support.

Note

1. Developmentally Appropriate Practice often shortened to DAP, is an approach to teaching grounded in the research on how young children develop and learn and in what is known about effective early education. (https://www.naeyc.org/DAP)

References

Ada, A. F. (2002). *I love Saturdays y domingos*. New York: Simon & Schuster.

Andrews, M., Squire, C., & Tamboukou, M. (2008). *Doing narrative research*. London: Sage.

Anzaldúa, G. (1997). *Friends from the other side/Amigos del otro lado*. San Francisco: Children's Book Press.

Banks, C. A. M., & Banks, J. A. (1995). Equity pedagogy: An essential component of multicultural education. *Theory into Practice, 34*(3), 152–158.

Bateson, G. (1988). *Mind and nature*. New York: Bantam.

Bloch, M. N. (2014). Interrogating *Reconceptualizing Early Care and Education* (RECE)— 20 years along. In M. N. Bloch, B. B. Swadener, & G. S. Cannella (Eds.), *Reconceptualizing early care and education: A reader* (pp. 19–31). New York: Peter Lang.

Bransford, J. D., Brown, A. L., & Cocking, R. R. (1999). *How people learn: Brain, mind, experience, and school*. Washington, DC: National Academies Press.

Bredekamp, S., & Copple, C. (Eds.). (1997). *Developmentally appropriate practice in early childhood programs* (rev. ed.). Washington, DC: National Association for the Education of Young Children.

Brown, C., & Lan, Y.-C. (2014). A qualitative metasynthesis of how early educators in international contexts address cultural matters that contrast with developmentally appropriate practice. *Early Education and Development, 26*(1), 22–45.

California Department of Education. (2012). *California State Common Core Standards*. Sacramento, CA: Author. Retrieved from http://www.cde.ca.gov/re/cc/

California Department of Education. (2014). *California preschool learning foundations*. Sacramento, CA: Author. Retrieved from http://www.cde.ca.gov/sp/cd/re/psfoundations.asp

Campbell, J. (2008). *The hero with a thousand faces (The collected works of Joseph Campbell)* (3rd ed.). New York: New World Library.

Carr, M., Duncan, J., Lee, W., Jones, C., Marshall, K., & Smith, A. (2009). *Learning in the making: Disposition and design in early education*. Rotterdam, Netherlands: Sense.

Cisneros, S. (1991). *The house on Mango Street*. New York: Vintage.

Dahlberg, G., Moss, P. M., & Pence, A. (2013). *Beyond quality in early childhood education and care: Languages of evaluation* (3rd ed.). New York: Routledge.

Eisler, R. (1988). *The chalice and the blade: Our history, our future*. New York: HarperOne.

Ely, M., Anzul, M., Friedman, T., Garner, D., & McCormack-Steinmetz, A. M. (1991). *Doing qualitative research: Circles within circles*. London: Falmer Press.

Freire, P. (1973). *Education for critical consciousness*. New York: Seabury.

Freire, P. (1984). *The politics of education: Culture, power, and liberation*. Granby, MA: Bergin & Garvey.

Freire, P. (1997). *Pedagogy of hope*. Granby, MA: Bergin & Garvey.

Giroux, H. (1988). *Teachers as intellectuals: Toward a critical pedagogy of learning*. New York: Praeger.

Kincheloe, J. (2000). Certifying the damage: Mainstream educational psychology and the oppression of children. In L. D. Soto (Ed.), *The politics of early childhood education* (pp. 75–84). New York: Peter Lang.

Kincheloe, J., McLaren, P., & Steinberg, S. R. (2012). Critical pedagogy and qualitative research: Moving to the bricolage. In S. R. Steinberg & G. S. Cannella (Eds.), *Critical qualitative research reader* (pp. 14–32). New York: Peter Lang.

Kincheloe, J., & Steinberg, S. (1998). *Changing multiculturalism*. Philadelphia: Open University Press.

Ladson-Billings, G. (2005). *Beyond the Big House: African American educators on teacher education*. New York: Teachers College Press.

Lee, C. D. (2008). The centrality of culture to the scientific study of learning and development: How an ecological framework in education research facilitates civic responsibility. *Educational Researcher, 37*(5), 267–279.

Lee, I. F., & Tseng, C. L. (2008). Cultural conflicts of the child-centered approach to early childhood education in Taiwan. *Early Years, 28*, 183–196.

Moll, L. C., Gonzalez, N., & Amanti, C. (2005). *Funds of knowledge: Theorizing practices in households, communities, and classrooms*. Mahwah, NJ: Lawrence Erlbaum Associates.

Nelson, K. (2009). *Young minds in social worlds: Experience, meaning, and memory*. Cambridge, MA: Harvard University Press.

New Zealand Ministry of Education. (Last updated March 2015.). *Pākōwhai Te Kōhanga Reo*. Retrieved from http://www.educate.ece.govt.nz/learning/curriculumAndLearning/Assessmentforlearning/TeWhatuPokekaEnglishLanguageVersion/PakowhaiTeKohangaReo.aspx

Pacini-Ketchabaw, V. (Ed.). (2010). *Flows, rhythms, and intensities of early childhood education curriculum*. New York: Peter Lang.

Penn, H. (2014). *Understanding early childhood: Issues and controversies* (3rd ed.). Berkshire, UK: Open University Press.

Pinar, W. (2004). *What is curriculum theory?* Mahwah, NJ: Lawrence Erlbaum Associates.

Polakow, V. (1989). Deconstructing development. *Journal of Education, 171*, 75–89.

Quintero, E. P. (2009a). *Critical literacy in early childhood education: Artful story and the integrated curriculum*. New York: Peter Lang.

Quintero, E. P. (2009b). *Refugee and immigrant family voices: Experience and education*. Rotterdam, Netherlands: Sense Publishers.

Quintero, E. P., & Rummel, M. K. (2003). *Becoming a teacher in the new society: Bringing communities and classrooms together*. New York: Peter Lang.

Ritchie, J., & Rau, C. (2009). Ma wai nga hua? "Participation" in early childhood in Aotearoa/New Zealand. *International Critical Childhood Policy Studies, 2*(1), 93–108.

Ritchie, J., & Rau, C. (2007). Ma wai nga hua? "Participation" in early childhood in Aotearoa/New Zealand. *International Journal of Educational Policy, Research and Practice: Reconceptualizing Childhood Studies, 8*(1), 101–116.

Rummel, Mary K., & Quintero, Elizabeth P. (1997). *Teachers' reading/teachers' lives*. Albany: SUNY Press.

Smith, S. (2012). *Early childhood mathematics*. Columbus, OH: Pearson.

Spencer, M. B. (2006). Phenomenology and ecological systems theory: Development of diverse groups. In W. Damon & R. M. Lerner (Eds.), *Handbook of child psychology* (6th ed., vol. 1, pp. 829–893). New York: John Wiley.

Taylor, A. (2013). *Reconfiguring the natures of childhood*. London: Routledge, Chapman & Hall.

Yoshikawa, H., Weiland, C., Brooks-Gunn, J., Burchinal, M. R., Espinosa, L. M., Gormley, W. T., ... Zaslow, M. J. (2013). Investing in our future: The evidence base on preschool education. Ann Arbor, MI: Society for Research in Child Development. Retrieved from http://www.srcd.org/policy-media/policy-updates/meetings-briefings/investing-our-future-evidence-base-preschool

· 3 ·

COMPLICATED CONVERSATIONS:
WHAT WE'RE LEARNING ABOUT
INTEGRATED CURRICULUM

Examples From the Complicated Conversations

It is important to reiterate here again that while the teacher education students participated in a listening, dialogue, action format framed by critical theory and Freire's (1985, 1997) work in their university classes, the format they used to write their activity/curriculum plans was adapted from a template used by transitional kindergarten programs in the state of California. As with many educational lesson planning approaches the required components, the order of presentation, and the terminology is often approach-specific. Because these student teachers are working with children ages 4 to 8, the lessons and therefore the format for presenting them by necessity bridge the early childhood approaches and the early elementary approaches. There were timely contextual events that influenced the decision about this aspect of the study, as mentioned at the end of Chapter 2. We made the decision to use this format after many discussions and analyses regarding the possibilities of our including our focus on critical theory while using the state's template for transitional kindergarten lesson planning. We decided (as bricoleurs) that we could use the format from the state of California transitional kindergarten's recommendation while remaining true to our intentions for critical integrated curriculum.

Furthermore, many of our collaborations are with early care and education professionals in the field who are in state-funded programs where teachers are required to adhere strictly to the *California Preschool Learning Foundations* in their practice, and they are not familiar with the listening, dialogue, action format of our critical literacy activity write-ups.

The *California Preschool Learning Foundations* promote key knowledge and skills that "…most children can achieve when provided with the kinds of interactions, instruction, and environments that research has shown to promote early learning and development" (California Department of Education, 2014). The foundations are intended to provide early childhood educators, parents, and the public with a clear understanding of the wide range of knowledge and skills that preschool children typically attain when given the benefits of a high-quality preschool program. The university early childhood studies students become very familiar with the state framework, discuss and analyze the field sites' use of the framework, and then in class discussions and through individual analysis, question the limitations and possibilities of the use of the framework (California Department of Education, 2014).

We decided that we could embed our critical ideas in the curriculum plans, with prominence, even using a more traditional template. Actually, among ourselves and in conversations in class discussions, we used the metaphors of scaffolding, subversive activity, and masquerade to analyze this decision. The student teachers in the past had had some limited success in their informal discussions with teachers in the field about the importance of the critical stances we have been taking in participatory curriculum creation and authentic assessment. Furthermore, it was interesting for the student teachers to use, with knowledge and understanding, the format with the state terminology, and to negotiate ways to challenge that with their alternative ways of thinking, doing, and labeling curriculum activities. Some cooperating teachers in the county programs were interested in this endeavor and gladly participated in the ongoing conversations in the field. Other teachers were not interested or not willing to veer away from the structured, scripted curriculum that some programs use.

Preschool Example

An early childhood studies student teacher, Ana,[1] placed in a state-funded preschool in our county, was very troubled at first about the differences between the preschool's philosophy and mandated curriculum and her own philosophy and practice. She was respectful, yet adamant, as she discussed her discontent in her journal:

> I have familiarized myself with the program guidelines and the teacher's thoughts about these guidelines. Along with this, I have also noted of the children's interests in the context of this program. In general, the program believes in the philosophy that a quality (no, they don't really have a concrete definition of quality) program should provide safe and high-performing early experiences for children ages 3 to 5 years. For this group of children, the teachers focus on preparing them for kindergarten. They follow two written curricula. The first curriculum is a set of educational materials for pre-K children by Abrams Learning Trends called "Let's Begin with the Letter People" (Abrams Learning Trends, n.d.). This set of materials and curriculum encompasses literacy skills in relation to the Common Core Standards. In addition to this set of materials, the program also follows math activities outlined in the book *Mathematics Their Way* (Baratta-Lorton, 1995). Together, these curriculum guidelines and the *California Preschool Learning Foundations* are assessed using the Desired Results Developmental Profile (DRDP). The teachers of the program believe that these guidelines are essential for preparing children for kindergarten. They follow them strictly, both in their teaching style and daily schedules. (Quintero, 2013, n.p.)

As explained earlier, in our early childhood studies program the student teachers are invited to revisit their own personal philosophies about supporting the learning and development of young children. And a nonnegotiable for us is the requirement that the student teachers observe and document the strengths, interests, needs, and complexities of the children they work with. In detail they describe what the children say, do, and struggle with, and what they know. And they must document, "How do you know they know that?"

The student teacher, Ana, reported:

> Despite the rigid schedule, I was able to observe shared interests among the children of both the morning and afternoon classes. I documented that the children showed continuous interest in wild animal life, insects, sports, and shared facts about their families....For example, I recorded that a small group of children playing at the block area were interested in wild animals; they immediately chose the animal figures to play with when building with the blocks. This same group later engaged in an imaginative play scenario where they pretended to be pigs, elephants and tigers. I would like to expand on this concept with this group of children with a planned activity.

> In addition to the interest in wild life, I have led children in discussions about their home life and sports while they are building houses with the blocks. From this unplanned activity, I have found that the children share an interest in sports, particularly soccer, and enjoy discussing their siblings. This gives me the idea that I can plan activities centering on physical activity, sports, and relatives. Since the

children's families are their first teachers, I feel it is important to allow the children to share information about them and document that information themselves to give them time to reflect. Lastly, sports and physical activity are integral parts of a child's development. The fact that the children in this program are showing an interest in this should be expanded on because it builds on their health and social needs. (Quintero, 2013, n.p.)

Astutely, she recognizes the importance of addressing the meaningful interests of the children while complying with the program guidelines. She discusses this dynamic:

In the mix of the teachers' expectations, program guidelines and curriculum, and the children's interests, this program always has a parent in the class to participate. The program firmly believes in parent participation and requires it as a part of enroll-ment. So far, I have gathered that parents desire their children to gain a formal and structured education from preschool. They hope for their children to be prepared for kindergarten in regards to literacy, mathematics, and all other areas of development. I would like to find out more about what the parents think about planning lessons in regards to the child's interests. I feel it is possible to integrate the programs belief in the preparation for later schooling with the child's interests in mind.

And finally, the student teacher adds her own articulation of her philosophy about young children's learning:

My personal belief about how children ages 4 to 8 years old [learn] go much deeper than the responses I got about this program's curriculum and standards. These beliefs stem from a number of philosophies and theorists, such as Vygotsky, and Malaguzzi. With these philosophies and theories in mind,…I believe children learn from having real-life experiences and when their interests from the environment are recognized. The people around them influence their thoughts, actions, and behaviors. Their environment and all living things affect how a child grows and develops. This culture provides a child with a set of beliefs that will impact every aspect of their learning. Children apply these beliefs to any new ideas presented to them and try to match what they are familiar with and what is new. As an educator, I feel this philosophy should be implemented when teaching and guiding children. Letting children freely explore their environment and have hands-on experiences is ideal in early childhood.

In addition to the above, I believe that young children learn best when their indi-vidual needs are taken into consideration. This includes providing children with the means to play and explore and providing a wide variety of materials to use. The role of the teachers is to facilitate children's learning and provide positive reinforcement. A supportive learning environment for young children is safe and stimulating and incorporates all cultures present in the classroom. Materials for children should be both age and experientially appropriate. The role of culture in children's learning is to show that they are represented and valued as a contributing member in the classroom. The role of parents and family in the children's learning is to be continuously involved in their children's education and development.

I deeply believe that the parents and family are the experts on their own children and are their first teachers. An effective early care and education program leader will allow open communication within the organization and community and be available and visible to everyone. This part of my philosophy is comparable to the program of my placement's philosophy because they believe in involving family, language, and culture.

Overall, I feel that my philosophy and curriculum ideas differ greatly from what I am seeing in my student teaching classroom. Many of their activities are pre-planned and require that children strictly follow a set schedule and planned activities. I believe that the schedule and activities should stem from what the children are interested in and allow room for spontaneous moments that veer off from the schedule. (Quintero, 2013, n.p.)

Fast-forward to the end of her semester, and an excerpt from the case study of her work shows that she was able to accommodate the program guidelines and the state standards while maintaining her allegiance to basing activities on the children's interests and strengths.

Preschool Integrated Curriculum, Lesson #1

Planned Topic: Changing weather means changing clothes

Age of Children: Pre-K

Big Idea: As the weather changes, we wear different types of clothes.

Child Input: What does she know? Who does she talk about? Who does she spend time with at home and at school?

During the morning class at the preschool, many of the children have noticed that the weather is changing from warm to cold. One day, I arrived wearing a heavy black coat and a child commented that my jacket was big. Throughout the day, children pointed out the cold weather attire that they were wearing, like a hooded Spiderman jacket or a princess long-sleeved shirt. Several children have commented on how their parents expressed that they need to wear warm clothes because it will be cold that day. This shows me that the children are aware of the weather and the proper clothes that need to be worn, as well as absorbing the comments their parents are making.

Integrated Areas of Study: art, literacy, science, social studies

Theme: Different types of clothes

Anchor Text: Teacher reads *The Rag Coat* by Lauren Mills (1991)

Project-Based Activity/ies:
A large group discussion on weather, season, and proper attire will occur. In addition, children will have the opportunity to engage in a small group activity where they will create their own art piece based on the literature presented.

Domain:
Early Childhood Development Domains (*California Preschool Learning Foundations*):

- Social-Emotional Development
- Cognitive Development
- Language/Linguistic Development
- Fine Motor Development

Content Area for K–3:

- English-Language Arts
- Visual Arts
- Science (specifically Earth Science)
- History/Social Sciences

Exploring Big Ideas in Large-Group Time

Procedure:
Children begin to notice that the weather is changing. It is nearing fall. A child is very interested in when it is going to be wintertime so he can wear the new coat that his mom bought him. Other children begin to talk about their fall/winter outerwear, like raincoats and thick snow jackets. One child confesses that he does not have a "coat." We discuss the different types of outwear, such as coats, parkas, raincoats, and sweaters.

Texts: (Children's literature, environmental print [multilingual] nonfiction texts and documents)

The Rag Coat by Lauren Mills (1991). Along with incorporating the idea of a coat in a child's life, this book teaches social-emotional themes of sharing, friendship, teasing, poverty, giving, death, forgiveness, and love. The illustrations and important lessons expose children to a different side of picture books.

Activity:
Building on idea and theme in small group and individually

Organization:
Dramatic Play Center: I bring in an old brown trench coat to place in the dramatic play area. The children take an interest in this because it has so many pockets and buttons.

Texts: (Children's literature, environmental print [multilingual] nonfiction texts and documents)
Reading/Library Center: Other texts with theme incorporated.

1. *The Purple Coat* by Amy Hest (1992): Every fall Gabrielle rides on the train and the subway with her mama to Grampa's tailor shop in New York City to be measured for a new navy blue coat. This year, however, she wants a purple coat. Grampa has a creative solution.
2. *One Little Lamb* by Elaine Greenstein (2004): Describes how a lamb's coat is made into yarn, which is made into mittens worn by a little girl when she visits the lamb on the farm.
3. *The Hungry Coat: A Tale from Turkey* by Demi (2004): After being forced to change to a fancy new coat to attend a party, Nasrettin Hoca tries to feed his dinner to the coat, reasoning that it was the coat that was the invited guest.
4. *Whose Coat?* by John Luksetich (2002): Aurora, looking for a coat in a department store, is told by a salesman where the coats come from. Aurora leaves, seeking the animals that gave up their coats, so she can take them to get their coats back.

Activity:
Tabletop Activity:
As an art activity, place scraps of clothing with glue and paper for children to construct their own fall/winter apparel. This is an art activity that could result in a collage from different materials. Children can also use scissors to cut their own pieces of fabric.

Evidence of Children Engaging with Concepts and People

Connect patterns of data from all activities:
What is next for these children? Why?

The children showed an interest in sharing information on their own winter attire. I may ask the children bring in their favorite coats, jackets, or winter attire to share with the class during language time. Also, many of the children showed an interest in the collage art project. I will provide the children with more opportunities to work with fabric materials through creating a class quilt and having these materials available for children to create their own designs.

Connections to family and community engagement for out-of-school possibilities:

The use of fabric in this activity leaves the possibility of family engagement open for several projects. Children can work with their families to collect their own scraps of fabric to create a quilt or "rag coat" together. They could also bring in fabric scraps that they found with their families to add to the class art materials.

Connections to goals and standards:

Engaging in art collage projects with their families expands on the standard of building empathy and kindness. Giving children the responsibility to bring in materials for the class to use shows an emerging sense of kindness. Also, using anchor texts that have a social justice theme builds on children's literature skills. Lastly, the children built on their self-awareness by sharing information about their own clothing and why they wear certain clothes for certain weather conditions.

Self-Reflection

This was the first lesson that I brought to participate with my preschool class. I was unsure if the children would understand the content of the anchor text *The Rag Coat*, but I felt that the overall message of the book should be shared. I decided to only read parts of the book. The children did react to the message, which was reflected in their art pieces. In addition to the large- and small-group activities, I also provided various types of coats and jackets for the children to explore in the dramatic play area. I feel that I could have connected these items to the lesson during the large-group activity. If I were to repeat this lesson, I would bring these items to the children's attention and discuss how it feels to wear each type of coat. I would then keep them available in the dramatic play area (Quintero, 2013, n.p.).

In Chapter 4, where I discuss our Storying Learning assessment, one Storying Learning example is by this student teacher, Ana, based on this lesson. The story will show that the lesson she and the children created and implemented has connections among the children, the philosophy of the student teacher, the integrated curriculum activity, the assessment method…and the children's learning.

Kindergarten/First Grade Example

Another early childhood studies student teacher in Southern California, Jen, was placed in a combination class of kindergarteners and first graders. In her case study she revealed that the staff of the school supported her in her experience, and they were required to insist that she needed to plan her experiences for the children using the California Common Core Standards for both kindergarten and first grade. She also included in her thinking and planning the influence of young children's histories, experiences, and language preferences as a part of the university class assignment. In addition, the classroom she was working in was required to adhere to the schoolwide, grade-level theme of their curriculum. The focus of the classroom's theme was a study of North America. In the student teacher's observations of the children, she learned that many are from Mexico and that many have relatives currently living in Mexico. So, a study of Mexico became part of her integrated curriculum work. She intentionally used children's literature and some informational texts that were nonfiction. It must be noted that the school and classroom teacher she was with used a much more teacher-directed style of curriculum implementation than the child-centered, collaborative, more postreconceptualist-influenced methods we had explored in the university classes. The student teacher and her cooperating teacher had a respectful relationship, and the student teacher felt she had some freedom to include child choice on some activities. On other activities, she was required to follow more closely the model used at the school.

She wrote in a journal entry as she was beginning to plan:

> Children are interested in describing and telling stories about their immediate surroundings. Children want to learn about their origins. Some say things like "I'm a Mexico person" or "I speak Mexican." Children are interested and curious about their

culture and how it defines, and is a part of, their identity. They enjoy sharing past times, traditions, and their ethnicity with others and me. They enjoy learning more about what is a part of them. (Quintero, 2013. n. p.)

She decided to use as her anchor texts *Abuela* by Arthur Dorros (English and Spanish editions, 1997), *Mexico, a True Book* by Ann Heinrichs (1997), and *Day of the Dead* by Tony Johnston and Jeanette Winter (2000). She planned project-based activities based on conversations with and observations of the children, and reported a synopsis of what happened:

We read, in a group read-aloud, *Mexico, a True Book*, and then in large group we created a vocabulary list together about the weather, physical environment, how people live, food, clothing, transportation and traditions. We discussed what things are similar and what things are different. Children usually focus on their immediate surroundings so I made sure to branch out about the geography, weather, traditions, and to ask questions that may trigger meaningful thought about family members who had moved to a different country or who had decided not to move.

We then broke up into small groups with a variety of activities:

- Group one: Children were supplied with materials to create artwork depictions of "One thing I'd like to do if I were in Mexico" and writing materials and paper to describe "One thing I'd like to do if I were in Mexico."
- Group two: Had choices of playing a game of Loteria or inventing and constructing a board game about Mexico.
- Group three: Worked on computers on a website relating to the geography of Mexico and map-making.
- Group four: Listened to a recording of words in Spanish that they often use in English. The children then attempted to have a conversation in Spanish using the correct terminology (with a native Spanish speaker). The children had the recording to refer back to as needed. (Quintero, 2013, n. p.)

Later that day, the student teacher read *Day of the Dead* (Johnston & Winter, 2000) and discussed the history of that celebration and why it's an important Mexican tradition. (She cited teacher-authored articles that she had found through *Rethinking Schools* that offered advice about ways to discuss the topic of death with young children in a variety of circumstances.) Then the children participated in an art project where they created a Day of the Dead collage.

The following day she brought in variety of different plants and pictures of animals that live and grow in Mexico. During group time with all the class together, she led the children in an informal study of the plants and animals. They discussed their names, passed the plants around, touched them, and described them. They talked about the animals in the pictures and discussed what they might need to survive. She then asked the children to pair up (one kindergartner and one first grader) and draw from a hat a piece of paper that had the name of either an animal or plant on it. The children worked together to draw or write descriptions of the animals or plants they had chosen.

Later that day, she read *Abuela* (Dorros, 1997) and led a group discussion about the different names we use in our families, depending on our language. The children had much to share about this "naming" in their families. Later, at some hastily created "listening centers," the children recorded their family stories about "naming."

Preliminary Findings and More Complicated Conversations

Through our research, findings emerged in three categories with respect to the use of story as an effective frame for critical integrated curriculum. The three categories of themes—(1) family story and symbolic play, (2) children's literature, and (3) children's writing—are illustrated in this chapter, along with examples from case studies of the critical, integrated curricula implemented with children. In Chapter 5, we discuss more complexities of overlapping findings about the policy, politics, and economics of early care and education provision. Of course, various content areas and learning domains surfaced through this model of integrated curriculum framed by critical literacy and personal story, and we were reminded over and over again that the broader systemic issues that encourage or constrain our day-to-day work couldn't be ignored.

Personal Story, Symbolic Play, and Integrated Curriculum

When young children dramatize their personal stories through pretend play, topics become layered with the complex issues regarding development and learning that must be discussed and addressed in education. Vivian Paley, during her decades of working with children in Chicago, documented the stories that children tell as part of their play and made them part of her daily curriculum. The stories consistently deal with issues of family and community and questions about fairness, justice, and what it means to be in school (Paley, 1986, 2000). Pretend and imaginative play is an important facet of young children's lives in terms of cognition and conceptual and emotional experiences. My own work (Quintero, 2002, 2004, 2009) in many multilingual, multicultural neighborhoods shows that throughout the play and engagement of "pretend" and symbolic story, children have opportunities for language use in home language, target language, and different forms of language. This language use that evolves naturally and holistically is an integral part of personal and communal story. Our understandings about story, the family history of young learners, and about language and literacy relate to the issue of home language use.

Unfortunately, much of the information publicized in the U.S. media, both about language and literacy of non–English-speaking people and about the best schooling programs for these students, is false. Students and their families who speak languages other than English can, and should, continue to nurture their home languages while their English acquisition is in progress. The languages and literacies enrich each other; they do not prohibit the students' becoming fluent and literate in English (Genesee, Paradis, & Crago, 2004; Magruder, Hayslip, Espinoza, & Matera, 2013). We are now certain that teachers and family members must support both the home language and English, or else dual-language learners can lose the ability to speak and understand their home language, or lose the balance between the two languages (Castro, Ayankoya, & Kasprzak, 2011).

The student teacher Jen, describing the children in the kindergarten/first-grade class, noted:

> Children are interested in describing and telling stories about their immediate surroundings. Children want to learn about their origin. Some say things like "I'm a Mexico person" or "I speak Mexican." Children are interested and curious about their culture and how it defines, and is a part of, their identity. They enjoy sharing past times, traditions, and their ethnicity with others and me. They enjoy learning more about what is a part of them. (Quintero, 2013, n.p.)

Teacher education students in this research often reflected on their own experiences of personal story and home language use in their own families and communities. The autobiographical opportunities inherent in critical literacy and integrated curriculum encourage students to tie their personal family stories to the learning situation of children learning English for the first time when they come to school. The following synopsis is from a case study of a teacher education student who implemented an integrated curriculum series of activities for a group of kindergarten children. She was interested in the broad issues of culture and identity as they relate to language and learning. She commented that the issue of meaning through language is important to her. Her case study reveals aspects of critical theory in terms of personal story/history, multiple sources of knowledge, and transformative action—with kindergarten students.

> A topic that has been of particular interest to me in early education has been that of responsiveness to family cultures, values, and languages. Having immigrated to the United States at a young age with my family, I have a personal connection with this topic. In my opinion, the incorporation of different cultures, values, and languages about each other's likenesses and differences via their culture, values, and languages should be a part of all teachers' curricula. Persons who come from different backgrounds can provide one another with new ideas or perspectives otherwise not explored. (Quintero, 2009, p. 73)

The student teacher wrote in a reflective journal about this group of learners:

> In this kindergarten class, out of the 24 students in the classroom, at least 12 were Dual Language Learners. Each student was at a different stage of learning the new language, English, and I had the opportunities to see and work with these students as they learned to read. (Quintero, 2009, p. 74)

She reflected on her integrated curriculum work with children about this topic so important to her own learning and living. She wrote:

> We can see the creation of new realities through the magical power of story, art and imagination. Children learn when they are exposed to historical information that relates to their own sense of place, families, and communities. There are many ways that students' ability to translate history into observation requires students to use a language that is not literal, that employs metaphor, illusion, and innuendo, and through story, students recognize that problems can have multiple solutions, questions can have multiple answers. (Quintero, 2009, p. 75)

It is important to think about this addressing of the cultural and historical identity intentions of this student teacher as a way to meaningfully include the children's worlds in the activities, as O'Laughlin (2009) advises:

> A minimal condition of depth pedagogy, therefore, is the reclamation of narrative threads and the location of children as subjects in history—people with genealogical

filiations, narrative continuity, and a possibility for becoming that is informed by, but not constrained by, ancestral, historical, and familial legacies. (O'Laughlin, 2009, p. 40)

There is a growing body of studies that use specific measures of brain activity that tap into the organization and functioning of language-relevant neural systems in ways that measures of young children's behaviors cannot. Together with studies of children's behaviors, including performance on tests and other structured tasks, the brain-imaging studies have led to the following conclusions:

1. Language experience affects the organization of the neural systems involved in learning, storing, processing, and producing language
2. Dual language learning and use involve some different cognitive processes than single language learning and use.
3. The effects of language learning experiences on the brain facilitate and constrain further learning, and these experiential effects may be what are often referred to as "critical period" effects in second language acquisition. (Conboy, 2011, p. 2)

These research findings emphasize the importance of integrated curriculum based on the children's interests, strengths, and needs, and making multilingual opportunities available. The brain's increasing specialization for processing the first language during early childhood does not necessarily limit its ability to learn another language: "Because the brain is not a limited capacity system, it can accommodate the learning of new information....Native language processing in early development was not adversely affected by exposure to another language" (Conboy, 2012, p. 32).

During play, children use their home language and often negotiate a new language if another child is a speaker of the new language in order to further their communication during the interaction. The most effective advice educators can give families is to let the natural ability of children to communicate take over. They can understand each other long before we adults can, and in a greater variety of ways. What is most important is that young children are exposed to an effective language-learning environment in an early childhood setting and at home.

Tania, a student teacher, wrote of a dramatic play event:

Today at preschool, I had the opportunity to interact with two 4-year-old girls who were playing in the sandbox. As I was walking around, they invited me over for some *posole* (a Mexican stew or soup). "Teacher Tania, Teacher Tania," they both hollered. "Do you want some *posole?*" As I walked over to the sandbox area, I instantly saw a bright red sand bucket with sand, sawdust bark (bark they had collected from the slide area), and water poured inside of it. After asking me again, I instantly replied, "I would love some *posole*." "YUM…YUM," I said with a big grin, "Does it come with cilantro and lime?" After shoveling more sand in the bucket, they replied, "Yup…we just added some." After all the ingredients were added, they then served me up some of their delicious (didn't look so delicious) soup with an actual soup spoon. Because I had grown up with Mexican food, I had to request one more food item that I love eating with my *posole*…corn tortillas. As I was shoveling down the *posole*, I asked, "Do you girls know how to make fresh homemade corn tortillas?" With a smile, one of the girls replied, "*Si*, my grandma makes me tortillas at home." With that, she took a sand sifter from one of the bins, pushed it into the sand in a circular motion. She made me scoop up the sand from the sifter and put it on a plate and said, "There you go, now eat!" After eating my *posole*, which was accompanied by a tortilla, they each started to talk about the other cultural dishes their families make them at home. After they talked about some of the dishes, I told them of some of the dishes I grew up with. In all, I would have to relate this experience to critical literacy that began with the children's play about creating a meal. These two girls were using oral language as a means to express and use story as a way of learning. (Quintero, 2013, n.p.)

Integrated Curriculum and Children's Literature

Children's literature, especially authentic and multicultural literature, provides opportunities for multilayered learning and sharing of histories. Bishop (1997) sees a two-faceted role for multicultural children's literature, serving as a mirror or a window. Children may see their own lives reflected in a story, or may have an opportunity see into others' lives. Multicultural literature incorporates the use of literary narrative and storytelling to challenge complex issues of race, historical authenticity, gender roles, and human responsibility. For example, in Faith Ringgold's *Tar Beach* (1996) and *Aunt Harriet's Underground Railroad in the Sky* (1995), the character Cassie uses her imagination and her stories to overcome oppression and limitations. Children, through their play, especially when immersed in an environment of literature and art, can provide us with voices and perspectives of possibility.

Ana, the student teacher who used the anchor text *The Rag Coat*, described earlier, wrote in her reflection:

[U]sing anchor texts that have a social justice theme builds on children's literature skills....I was unsure if the children would understand the content of the anchor text, *The Rag Coat*, but I felt that the overall message of the book should be shared. I decided to only read parts of the book. The children did react to the message, which was reflected in their art pieces. (Quintero, 2013, n.p.)

Children's literature author Lise Lunge-Larsen reminds us in the introduction to one of her books of the importance of literature and folk tales in children's lives:

Children, like the heroes and heroines in these stories, perceive their lives to be constantly threatened. Will I lose a tooth? Will I be invited to play? Will I learn to read? By living a life immersed in great stories and themes, children will see that they have the resources needed to solve life's struggles. And, while listening to these stories, children can rest for a while in a world that mirrors their own, full of magic and the possibility of greatness that lies within the human heart. (1999, p. 11)

Another case study from a pilot to this study documents a lesson in a first-grade classroom in an urban school in a large city and illustrates the importance of home language use and multicultural literature. The teacher and student teacher both believed in the importance of history, family, and community, and the importance of young children connecting their histories with stories in literature. The teacher was a 20-year veteran teacher with the district, a woman of Irish American descent. The student teacher with her was a Hmong male who is from the community where the school is situated. The students in the class consisted of sixteen Hmong children, three African American children, and one child from South America. For this lesson, the teacher used the storybook *Whispering Cloth: A Refugee's Story* by Pegi Deitz Shea (1995).

The teacher began by gathering the children around her in the classroom center area, where she unfolded several quilts. She reminded them of previous discussions and stories they had shared about quilts. Then she showed a weaving from Ireland and explained that it was from the country her family came from. Then, she held up a large, colorful "storycloth" that had been made by one of the school staff's relatives, who is Hmong.

The teacher asked, "Do you think a quilt could tell a story? Do you think you can hear a story from a cloth?" After the children discussed briefly what they thought about the question, the teacher passed the folded cloth around the circle, so that each student could "listen" to the cloth. Then, she showed the class the book *The Whispering Cloth*, and told them just a little about the book.

"It is a story about a Hmong girl and her grandmother who live in a refugee camp in Thailand. Grandmother is teaching Mai how to make storycloths and Mai creates one that tells her story."

Then the teacher showed the bilingual glossary in the book with Hmong words and English translations, and explained that she would read the story in English in a few minutes, but first, the student teacher would read it in Hmong.

The story was read in Hmong. The students who did not understand Hmong appeared to be fascinated by the words in spite of not comprehending them. The teacher then asked the children whether they could guess what the story was about based upon his intonations, the pictures, and so forth. Then the teacher read the story in English.

During choice time, the children went to centers where they could begin drawing a storycloth and documenting the history it told. The geography center had maps and storybooks showing Laos and other Southeast Asian countries. There was a language center with a tape of a story being read in Hmong, and a writing center where children could write questions to ask family and community members about their migration history.

At the close of the day, the student teacher explained to the students that he had written a letter to their families explaining what they were learning about. The letter was written in English, Hmong, and Spanish. In the letter, the teachers ask the parents whether their child could share a storycloth, quilt, or an artifact that tells a family story. When the items were brought to school, extension activities were implemented. The students made a class storycloth with a contribution from each student's drawing and writing (native language or English or both) during the following days (Quintero, 2009).

Alma Flor Ada emphasizes that children's literature can be a window into the families, cultures, and experiences of children (Ada & Campoy, 2003). Writer and poet Gloria Anzaldúa makes an even stronger statement about children's literature:

> I also want Chicano kids to hear stuff about la Llorona, about the border, et cetera, as early as possible. I don't want them to wait until they are 18 or 19 to get that information. I think it is very important that they get to know their culture already as children. Here in California I met a lot of young Chicanos and Chicanas who didn't have a clue about their own Chicano culture…later on, when they were already 20, 25, or even 30 years old, they took classes in Chicano studies to learn more about their ancestors, their history and culture. But I want the kids to already have access to this kind of information. That is why I started writing children's books. (Ikas, K. 2003)

When discussing the importance of children's literature and picture books for learning, Anzaldúa elaborates:

> An image is a bridge between evoked emotion and conscious knowledge; words are the cables that hold up the bridge. Images are more direct, more immediate than words, and closer to the unconscious. Picture language precedes thinking in words; the metaphorical mind precedes analytical consciousness. (Anzaldúa, 1999, p. 91)

Illustrating this point, Jen, the student teacher in the kindergarten/first grade classroom when working with the children on activities related to Mexico discussed reading *Abuela* (Dorros, 1997). She led a group discussion about the different names we use in our families depending on language. The children had much to say about this "naming" in their families. Later, at some "listening centers" the children recorded their family stories about "naming." And this lead to writing about the family stories focusing on "naming." This writing is significant because of the dynamic deep meaning for the children and the families.

Integrated Curriculum and Children's Writing

Scholars who are critical theorists believe that the "texts" students and teachers "decode" should contain images of their own concrete, situated experiences with their friends, their families, and communities. This is a way to radically redefine conventional notions of print-based literacy and conventional school curriculum. This does not mean throwing out, or ignoring, or not providing access to accepted bodies of information and the canon in learning events. It means sharing the space, the time, and especially the importance of the old and the new. Even very young children are experts at writing about their worlds.

It has been found that children, with encouragement and acceptance, do gain self-confidence to do their own reading and writing. They will voice their own reality in terms of culture, social issues, and cognitive development when it is valued as a sharing of knowledge (Quintero, 2004). Teachers can create classroom contexts in which all students can use their voices to affirm their social contexts and to create new situations for themselves through writing. The work of Donald Graves (1994) and his colleagues suggests that three conditions are necessary for children to make progress as writers. First, they must be allowed and encouraged to write on topics they really care about, with the expectation that their work will be read seriously for its content. After all, why should they sustain the effort of writing and revising if they are not personally involved with their topics, or do not expect to be read? Second, there is a fluid aspect to writing growth. Children need time and frequent practice to get better at writing. Third, children need sensitive guidance from adults to become good writers. Further research over the past twenty years based on Graves's initial findings continues to demonstrate these ideas about children's writings (Calkins, 1994; Calkins, Ehrenworth, & Lehman, 2012; Fletcher, 2001; Strickland, 2010.) An important question is, why are these ideas and findings about young children's writing considered to be so radical?

In cases with young children, an integrated approach with a critical literacy framework can enrich curriculum and keep the student-centered integrity and provide the scaffolding needed for younger learners. This methodology, with its strong theoretical and philosophical underpinnings, encourages teachers not to limit their teaching to units and lesson plans. It encourages teachers to use as a point of departure the background funds of knowledge the children bring from their lived experiences rather than from a written form of normalization. The method encourages integration of the community funds of knowledge, language, and culture with the standard school curricula.

In a discussion about story dictation of young preschoolers, Daitsman (2009) cites advice from Stribling and Kraus (2007) about challenging the linear model of thinking of early writing as simply a matter of learning the mechanics of writing. Stribling and Kraus, according to Daitsman, encourage teachers to favor "a more complex approach that encourages young writers to explore content at the same time they are making sense of mechanics" (2009, p. 15). Meier (2009) says, "Children are the ones who know how to do everything with stories 'altogether.' Children know that there is no other way" (pp. 163–164).

Another case documents problem-posing in kindergarten, with Van Gogh's *The Bedroom in Arles* (or *Vincent's Bedroom in Arles*). The student teacher brought to the classroom a print she had bought from the Vincent Van Gogh Museum in Amsterdam. She sat in a rocking chair on the rug with the print rolled up in a cardboard case as the children gathered. Some of the children noticed the word *museum* on the case and predicted that it was a painting. She took out the print and showed the class *The Bedroom in Arles*. She then shared with the children a letter Van Gogh had written to his brother, which she had found on the museum's website. The letter said,

My eyes are still tired by then I had a new idea in my head and here is the sketch of it. Another size 30 canvas. This time it's just simply my bedroom, only here colour is to do everything, and giving by its simplification a grander style to things, is to be suggestive here of rest or of sleep in general. In a word, looking at the picture ought to rest the brain, or rather the imagination. (Harrison, 2001)

She put the print of the painting on an easel and asked the children to look at it for a few minutes. She then asked them to think about how they would draw or write a response to the painting.

Before they began their creations, the student teacher shared her response, which was a poem she had written titled "My Bed." Then she gave out pencils and blank pieces of paper and told the children to go wherever they wanted in the classroom with their writing tools and create a response to the painting.

The children drew pictures of their own bedrooms and wrote about the things in the room and/or what they do there. Some children wrote a question they had about the painting, such as "Whose room is this?" Some of the comments (with invented spelling) they wrote were:

"BEDS R SAOFT AND RWOM" (Beds are soft and warm.)

"MY LAME IS CIDE. I SLIP WITH HR AVR NIT" (My lambie is cuddly. I sleep with her every night)

"I LOVE MY BED I SLEEP WITH MY DOLL SARAH. MY MOM SINGS SONGS. I LOVE MY BED." (Quintero, 2009, p. 150)

The student teacher reported also that

One child drew a picture of himself in his room and explained to me the items in it. He showed me the blanket all around him, his apple, reading lamp and ladder.

One child was compelled to write a heartfelt song filled with well wishes. "I WISH, I MAY, I WISH, I MIT (might), HAVE THE WISH TONIT (tonight), I WISH, YOU SEEP (sleep) WEL AND HOPE I DO TO (too)." (Quintero, 2009, p. 150)

She reflected that "seeing and hearing them problem-pose, critically think about art, and write their thoughts culminated the activity" (Quintero, 2009, pp. 149–150).

Another student teacher, Pam, was placed in a state-funded preschool in Southern California. Although a large percentage of the children are Spanish-speaking and just learning English for the first time, the school does

not support the use of home languages except in emergencies or when speaking with parents. The student teacher, herself a bilingual California native,
was in the sensitive position of trying to almost subversively support the
4-year-olds' use of their home language. As she was collecting observation
data for her integrated curriculum lesson planning, she became friends with
a child we will call Fernando. She wrote a lengthy journal report about the
child, the situation, and his writing potential through pretend play and his
wish to use his home language.

> I am assigned to sit with 4-year-old Fernando, who is unable to sit down on the rug
> during literacy time. Since he is unable to control his behavior, and sit quietly cross-
> ing his legs (that all children are requested to do). Fernando is told to sit in a chair.
>
> Fernando shows interest in my notebook as soon as he notices I am writing notes. He
> wants to write his name. "Fernando, you may write your name as soon as we go out
> and play. Let's listen to Teacher right now."
>
> "Yo escribo mi nombre?" (Do I write my name?) he asks me in Spanish. "Si, despues
> que salgamos a jugar afuera" (Yes, after we go to play outside), I answer him back in
> Spanish. "Ok Teacher. Gracias." He turns to listen to his other teacher.
>
> As soon as we are outside during play time, Fernando runs up to me, "Teacher Pam,
> yo hago homework" (Teacher Pam, I do homework). "You do your homework?" I
> ask. "No! Tu homework!" (No, your homework!). He wants to do MY homework.
> I give him my notepad, unsure what he means. He begins writing. He writes, then
> looks up, around, then writes some more. He is pretending to do the same work
> that I do. Finally I realize, this boy, who seems to encounter behavioral problems,
> does not listen and follow directions, cannot manage to sit still with his peers, has
> been observing me. He has noticed I take notes and imitates me doing homework.
> (Quintero, 2014, p. 183)

This brings us to student writing and the creation of texts and opportunities for the growing number of dual-language learners in our programs. Many
researchers and practitioners maintain that learners develop their knowledge of second-language writing and speaking conventions by using what
they understand about writing in their home language. Many researchers and
classroom teachers have shown that language interaction in the form of student-centered discussions and demonstrations, language experience story writing and reading, and holistic literacy development allow for home-language
literacy to enhance English-language literacy development. Research shows
(Castro et al., 2011; Genesee, 2010) that dual-language learners benefit from

instruction that focuses on decoding and comprehension in English. Research also shows that a strong home-language base makes it easier to learn English, and that young children can learn two languages as naturally as learning one (Associated Press, 2009; Bialystok, 2009).

While early childhood educators understand that oral language development is a critical component of later reading success, the strategies for supporting this link between oral language/s and written language/s are often left out of teacher development. Integrated curriculum helps to bridge the strategy gaps for all children, and especially for dual-language learners.

We write what we notice, and in the process of writing, notice more, discover more. Our own voices become stronger the closer we come to what's critically important to us and what unleashes our own emotions. The literacy endeavor in children's writing involves both individual transformations and transformations in context of various groups of people. If we want to encourage children to use language to create new images for themselves in cultural contexts, we must guide children's voices through reading and writing in expressive genres like fiction, poetry, and creative nonfiction. We can teach children to tune in to the voices of the writers they read and to listen to voices of their own lives.

An integrated approach to supporting young learners and dual-language learners has been proven effective (Magruder et al., 2013) and adapted for use in the current study. This integrated approach includes: print-rich labeling in English and all children's home languages; books, materials, displays, and artifacts reflecting all languages, cultures, families, and communities of children; anchor texts; vocabulary imprinting (use of photographs, images, and word walls to introduce new concepts and vocabulary and deepen comprehension); visual cues/gestures; and center extensions.

There is not enough discussion and exploration in teacher education circles regarding ways in which native language writing can be used to enhance multiliteracy instruction (Matera, Armas, & Lavandenz, 2013). Some of the most convincing evidence of alternative theoretical propositions regarding bilingual writing comes from research of dual-language or two-way bilingual immersion programs (Cummins, 2000). The contextual reality of many English literacy classrooms in the United States and all over the world is that a large variety of native languages are present. It is almost always impossible for each teacher to be knowledgeable of every language represented in the classroom. Reyes (1992, 2011) and Quintero (2002) document that is it rarely crucial for the classroom teacher to be proficient in all languages represented by students in the classroom. Yet, by using integrated curriculum, any classroom teacher can orchestrate meaningful lessons that include writing in the students' home language.

Reflections

Finally, evaluation of the effectiveness of methodology created with a qualitative focus and such variety of contexts and participants is difficult. As the adult participants engaged with story in their own learning, they used this learning to scaffold their collaboration, design and implementation of early childhood curriculum that supported children's learning, and the findings regarding story as it related to critical theory structured the analysis. The complicated conversations of the integrated curriculum case studies show a culturally and developmentally responsive way to address integration of content area study in early learning. And as student teacher Bree, who had engaged children with Van Gogh's work, said, "seeing and hearing them problem-pose, critically think about art, and write their thoughts culminated the activity."

Note

1. Names changed to protect privacy.

References

Abrams Learning Trends. (n.d.). *Land of the Letter People*. Retrieved from https://www.abramslearningtrends.com/products/land-letter-people

Ada, A. F., & Campoy, I. (2003). *Authors in the classroom: A transformative educational process*. New York: Pearson.

Anzaldúa, G. (1999). *Borderlands/La frontera: The new mestiza* (2nd ed.). San Francisco: Spinsters/Aunt Lute Press.

Associated Press. (2009, July 20). *Unraveling how kids become bilingual so easily*. Retrieved from http://www.nbcnews.com/id/32013276/#.VK6lG02zVjo

Baratta-Lorton, M. (1995). *Mathematics their way*. New York: Dale Seymour Publications.

Bialystok, E. (2009). Bilingualism: The good, the bad, and the indifferent. *Bilingualism: Language and Cognition, (12)*1, 3–11.

Bishop, R. S. (1997). Selecting literature for a multicultural curriculum. In V. Harris (Ed.), *Using multiethnic literature in the K–8 classroom* (pp. 1–19). Norwood, MA: Christopher-Gordon Publishers.

California Department of Education. (2014). *California preschool learning foundations*. Retrieved from http://www.cde.ca.gov/sp/cd/re/psfoundations.asp

Calkins, L. (1994). *The art of teaching writing*. Portsmouth, NH: Heinemann.

Calkins, L., Ehrenworth, M., & Lehman, C. (2012). *Pathways to the Common Core*. Portsmouth, NH: Heinemann.

Castro, D. C., Ayankoya, B., & Kasprzak, C. (2011). *New voices/Nuevas voces: Guide to cultural and linguistic diversity in early childhood*. Baltimore, MD: Brookes.

Conboy, B. (2011). *Impact of second-language experience in infancy: Brain measures of first- and second-language speech perception*. Seattle, WA: Institute for Learning & Brain Sciences, University of Washington.

Conboy, B. (2012). Research techniques and the bilingual brain. In C. A. Chappelle (Ed.), *The encyclopedia of applied linguistics* [online]. New York: John Wiley & Sons. Retrieved from http://onlinelibrary.wiley.com/doi/10.1002/9781405198431.wbeal1010/pdf

Cummins, J. (2000). *Language, power, and pedagogy: Bilingual children in the crossfire*. Clevedon, UK: Multilingual Matters.

Daitsman, J. (2009). Once upon a time there was a...: Forms and functions of story dictation in preschool. In D. Meier (Ed.), *Here's the story: Using narrative to promote young children's language and literacy learning* (pp. 109–122). New York: Teachers College Press.

Demi. (2004). *The hungry coat: A tale from Turkey*. New York: Margaret K. McElderry Books.

Dorros, A. (1997). *Abuela /Grandmother*. New York: Puffin.

Fletcher, R. (2001). *Writing workshop: The essential guide*. Portsmouth, NH: Heinemann.

Freire, P. (1985). *The politics of education*. Granby, MA: Bergin & Garvey.

Freire, P. (1997). *Pedagogy of hope*. Granby, MA: Bergin & Garvey.

Genesee, F. (2010). Dual language development in preschool children. In E. E. Garcia & E. Frede (Eds.), *Young English language learners: Current research and emerging directions for practice and policy* (pp. 59–79). New York: Teachers College Press.

Genesee, F., Paradis, J., & Crago, M. B. (2004). *Dual language development and disorders: A handbook on bilingualism and second language learning*. Baltimore, MD: Brookes.

Graves, D. (1994). *A fresh look at writing*. Portsmouth, NH: Heinemann.

Greenstein, E. (2004). *One little lamb*. New York: Viking.

Harrison, R. G. (2001). *Letter 554. Arles, 16 October 1888. The Bedroom in Arles*. *http://www.vggallery.com/letters/683_V-T_554.pdf*

Heinrichs, A. (1997). *Mexico, a true book*. Danbury, CT: Children's Press.

Hest, A. (1992). *The purple coat*. New York: Aladdin.

Ikas, K. (2003). Interview with Gloria Anzaldúa who discusses her motivation for *This Bridge Called My Back*. (http://www.auntlute.com/www.auntlute.com/auntlute.com/GloriaAnzalduaInterview.htm)

Johnston, T., & Winter, J. (2000). *Day of the dead*. New York: HMH Books for Young Readers.

Luksetich, J. (2002). *Whose coat?* New York: Imagine Nation Press.

Lunge-Larsen, L. (1999). *The troll with no heart in his body and other tales of trolls from Norway.* Boston: Houghton Mifflin.

Magruder, E., Hayslip, W., Espinoza, L., & Matera, C. (2013). Many languages, one teacher: Supporting language and literacy development for preschool dual language learners. *Young Children, 68*(1), 8–15.

Matera, C., Armas, E., & Lavandenz, M. (2013, spring). Dialogic reading and the development of transitional kindergarten teachers' expertise with dual language learners. *The Multilingual Educator, 37*–40. Retrieved from http://www.bilingualeducation.org/ME/ME2013.pdf

Meier, D. (2009). *Here's the story: Using narrative to promote young children's language and literacy learning.* New York: Teachers College Press.

Mills, L. (1991). *The rag coat.* New York: Little, Brown Books for Young Readers.

O'Laughlin, M. (2009). *The subject of childhood.* New York: Peter Lang.

Paley, V. G. (1986). *Boys and girls: Superheroes in the doll corner.* Chicago: University of Chicago Press.

Paley, V. G. (2000). *White teacher.* Cambridge, MA: Harvard University Press.

Quintero, E. P. (2002). A problem-posing approach to using native language writing in English literacy instruction. In S. Ransdell & M. L. Barbier (Eds.), *Psycholinguistic approaches to understanding second language writing* (pp. 34–46). Dordrecht, Netherlands: Kluwer Press

Quintero, E. P. (2004). What you didn't know about diversity and education. In J. Kincheloe & S. Steinberg (Eds.), *12 things you didn't know about schools* (pp. 211–222). New York: Palgrave.

Quintero, E. P. (2009). *Critical literacy in early childhood education: Artful story and the integrated curriculum.* New York: Peter Lang.

Quintero, E. P. (2013). Research journal. unpublished manuscript.

Quintero, E. P. (2014). Juan, Melina, and friends: Guides for reconceptualizing readiness. In W. Parnell & J. M. Iorio (Eds.), *Reconceptualizing readiness in early childhood education* (pp. 179–190). New York: Springer.

Reyes, M. de la Luz. (1992). Questioning venerable assumptions: Literacy instruction for linguistically different students. *Harvard Education Review, 2*(4), 427–444.

Reyes, M. de la Luz. (2011). *Words were all we had: Becoming biliterate against the odds.* New York: Teachers College Press.

Ringgold, F. (1995). *Aunt Harriet's underground railroad in the sky.* New York: Crown Publishers.

Ringgold, F. (1996). *Tar beach.* New York: Dragonfly Books.

Shea, P. D. (1995). *Whispering cloth: A refugee's story.* Honesdale, PA: Boyds Mill Press.

Stribling, S. M., & Kraus, S. (2007). Content and mechanics: Understanding first grade writers. *Voices of Practitioners, 2*(2), 1–17.

Strickland, D. (2010). *Essential readings on early literacy.* Newark, DE: International Reading Association.

· 4 ·

ASSESSMENT IN EARLY CHILDHOOD: STORYING LEARNING

Storying Learning Over Time

As we have maintained throughout this study, and as I opened this book by saying, early childhood teacher education is about young children's learning, young children's learning to learn, and the social and cultural contexts where this learning takes place. It is also about the people and the human aspects that support this learning. For these reasons, an integrated approach to curriculum is paramount. And, finally, an assessment system that documents the complicated process over time with a collaboration of families, children, teachers and researchers is of utmost importance, so that we may continually learn about the learning. Qualitative data featuring the voices of the children and the people important in their worlds give shared meaning to quantitative data being analyzed by policy makers in current international discussions about curriculum, assessment, and quality. My certainty about this stance regarding the importance of collecting documentation over time through collaboration of families, children, and educators is confirmed by research and practice.

We have realized as we have studied the work of New Zealand early care and education researchers and teachers over the past several years that we can borrow and adapt some of the intellectual, academic, collaborative, and practice-based structures that they have been using and perfecting for the past decades. These professionals have created a responsive (to children and families, culture, and language) and research-based curriculum and an assessment system that is linked foundationally and practically to the curriculum they have created. We see these contributions as guides for our providing a positive model of learning support that doesn't pit learners against each other as they traverse their educational journeys. Our model will not be continually subject to objectives and accountability measures set by top-down mandates, but will support collaborative and individual learning and document the journey in an authentic way.

The New Zealand researchers base their curriculum on learning dispositions, defined as "complex units of educational input, uptake and outcome" (Carr et al., 2009, p. 15). They say, "We are more or less disposed to notice, recognize, respond to, reciprocate with, author, improvise from, and imagine alternatives to, what we already know and can do" (Carr et al., 2009, p. 15). These dispositions identified are akin to goals or standards agreed upon and negotiated through a process of collaboration by the original participants of professionals and parents creating the *Te Whāriki* curriculum. Carr et al. (2009) address the importance of thinking about children's learning in all aspects of their lives:

> The cultures that develop in early childhood centres and school classrooms can be described as "dispositional milieux"; they may be overt and public, or subtle and covert; they may support the spirit and intent of a curriculum document or they may not....We suggest that learning dispositions are features of places, in the case of early childhood centres, school classrooms and homes. These dispositional milieux are affordance networks: networks of useful resources, including people, that provide, *or appear to provide*, opportunities and constraints for the learning that the individual has in mind. (p. 8)

It is important to bring in Bloch (2014) again, as we think about curriculum work in the vast variety of community contexts in the United States and in a variety of international contexts.

> [W]hose voices and knowledge count? Whose values are embedded in what we think is appropriate curriculum and for whom? Critical questions and some responses are illustrated...in the critically significant work of the Maori/non-Maori researchers participation in the development and continued critique of the *Te Whāriki* early childhood curriculum (originally published in 1997; Ritchie & Rau, 2009)... The mental research (Pacini-Ketchabaw, 2010; Taylor, 2013) that has allowed for

the imagining of the "natures" of the child with/in his/their ecological and cultural context has added powerful dimensions to possibilities for curriculum theory and pedagogy. (p. 24)

Final Reflection Responses From Ana

The student teacher Ana, whose integrated lesson plan about changing weather and coats was detailed in Chapter 3, wrote a reflection at the end of the semester that is included in her case study. The student teachers had been asked to connect the "input" they learned from their first observations of children they work with, to the guidelines and standards used by the program where they were participating, and to their experience with "Storying Learning" assessments from their university class. She wrote:

1. Describe the child input from earlier observations influencing your lesson/activity planning.

During the morning class at the preschool, many of the children have noticed that the weather is changing from warm to cold. One day, I arrived wearing a heavy black coat and a child commented that my jacket was big. Throughout the day children pointed out the cold weather attire that they were wearing, like a hooded Spiderman jacket or a "princess" long sleeve shirt. Several children have commented on how their parents expressed that they need to wear warm clothes because it will be cold that day. This showed me that the children were aware of the weather and the proper clothes that need to be worn, as well as absorbing the comments their parents are making about the weather.

2. Illustrate the connection between the child's "funds of knowledge" and your curriculum activities.

Child C gave constant input on the new jacket that his mom bought him for the snow and cold weather. His mom is an avid volunteer for the school and works part-time for the school library. She frequently comes to check on him. During the day of this lesson, Child C's mom came in after he finished his art project. He was excited to share with her that he dressed up his "person" so he could be warm. I walked over to explain the activity, and Child C made it known that he had a really cool new jacket. I asked if he could wear it to school, but his mom explained it was a little too heavy for the weather, considering it was a snow jacket. Child C's family often visits relatives who experience snowy weather. This showed me that Child C is very familiar with extreme cold winter climates, which may be why he was so empathetic to the young girl in the story who did not have a coat.

3. Use this same child input connecting to one or more of the standards/guidelines you used.

Child C quickly learned the theme of the story and lesson. In his artwork and comments on making a coat so his "person" can stay warm, Child C reflected the California Preschool Learning Foundations regarding empathy, caring, and social and emotional understanding. These standards specify that children over 60 months of age should begin to comprehend the mental and psychological reasons people act as they do and how they contribute to differences between people. In addition, the standard defining empathy and caring in regard to preschool-age children states that they should be able to respond to another's distress and needs with sympathetic caring and are more likely to assist. Child C's actions in the making of his art project and during the reading of the anchor text show these skills emerging.

4. Discuss your own learning and professional growth (you may use one or more of the Learner Outcomes on our syllabus) as a result of the *total experience* of using *child input*, designing *integrated curriculum*, and writing *Storying Learning assessments*.

From my total experience of using child input, designing integrated curriculum, and writing Storying Learning, I have grown to understand this process at a deeper level as well as learned to apply my knowledge in different ways. When reflecting on my integrated curriculum designs after beginning the process with the children at my student teaching site, I was able to apply additional California Preschool Foundation standards that I did not initially intend for the children to develop. Without this process of learning stories and reflections, I would not have seen what I could improve on in the future with my lessons, and what standards I could integrate into the lesson. In addition, I learned how valuable child and family input is to the child's learning process. I have become more attuned to these factors and now use them as the basis of collaborating with the children and teachers about the lessons. (Quintero, 2013, n.p.)

This student's responses illustrate a growing trend: Based upon our research and practice, it appears that the participating early childhood teacher education students have begun to seriously question issues of assessment for young children.

Are We Asking the Right Questions Regarding Assessment?

We continually ask, is it possible to support collaborative and individual learning and document the journey in an authentic way? While studying the guidelines and assessments that are currently used in many state- and federally funded programs, the participants in this study have been committed to implementing assessments that are collaborations of teachers, families, and children.

After reading a few vignettes, such as those about Melina in Chapter 1 and Child C above, university students were asked to view introductory information about the way assessment is approached by early childhood education in New Zealand. In response, the student teacher above, Ana, said:

> What stood out to me most was that assessment should be reflecting activities and everyday practice. My site [where she is student teaching] seems to be doing very "old school" types of assessment. A child will be pulled from class, taken to another room, sat down, and asked questions. This can be terrifying for children. I know it was for me. Teachers are taking time out of the day to complete endless checklists, etc., while the children are engaging in activities. An alternative, more authentic, type of assessment could be as easy as listening in on a conversation of two children about a sorting activity and hearing their knowledge and take on the topic. (Quintero, 2013, n.p.).

Another student teacher in our case studies, Celeste, wrote about a complex situation (often very typical in early childhood programs) that involved many issues of assessment, including the use of home languages for dual-language learners:

> At the Children's Center, the home language of, if not all, most, children is Spanish. When I go in to do my fieldwork, I am submerged in this language, by the children and the two teacher's aides; I have not heard the teacher speak it, but she can understand it. Spanish is my home language as well, and it was my first language, so I feel very comfortable talking to the children in Spanish. I find myself talking to the children in Spanish more than in English because they ask me something or talk to me in Spanish so I reply in Spanish.

> I observed a situation in Spanish toward the end of project time. The lead teacher's project for the children was coloring an oval with the shade that the children thought was like their skin color. Every day they were going to add a different feature to the face until they were done with the complete face.

> Towards the end of the project, two girls mentioned in Spanish that they were going to go to the dramatic play area and wear the *zapatillas*, which were the slippers. One of them told the other that she couldn't wear them because she was going to save the other pair for another friend. They have to get excused from the work group by the teacher first, so they were both trying to get the teacher's attention so they could leave. The teacher excused the girl who had said that she was going to save the other slippers for a friend, and so she ran to go get both pairs. At that point, the other girl started crying and saying that she wanted to wear the slippers. The teacher, as

I mentioned before, doesn't speak Spanish, and even though the girl's conversation was in Spanish, she told them, "I see that both of you want the slippers but if she already got both pairs you can wait. What is the rule with the slippers?" They then answered, "Five minutes," and the teacher said, "Okay, so she has 5 minutes with both pairs." The girl that didn't get the slippers was still crying and saying that she wanted the slippers, while the other one told her friend to hurry up so she can get excused from the table so they could play. This whole conversation between all three girls was in Spanish. (Quintero, 2013, n.p.)

This story involving day-to-day challenges of sharing, respecting rules, and getting along in a group shows how home language and the language of the teachers must be bridged. And this story prompted our early childhood studies students to ask questions about our ability to do reliable assessments if we don't use the children's home language for that assessment. This brief vignette brings up specific aspects of assessment issues, such as language use, and other more general issues of assessment.

Selected Examples of Early Childhood Assessments Used in the United States

On a national basis, there are several initiatives to implement assessments in early childhood settings that are meant to be developmentally and culturally appropriate. For many of us in the field, the initiatives are lacking in many ways. Two frequently used assessments will be briefly discussed to illustrate some aspects of the current assessments in use. One assessment is the Early Childhood Environment Rating Scale (ECERS). The ECERS provides an overall picture of the surroundings that have been created for the children and adults who share an early childhood setting. The ECERS consists of 43 items that assess the quality of the early childhood environment, including use of space, materials, and experiences to enhance children's development, daily schedule, and supervision.

The ECERS evaluates personal care routines, space and furnishings, language-reasoning, activities, interactions, program structure, parents, and staff on a scale from 1 to 7. A ranking of 1 indicates inadequate conditions, whereas a ranking of 7 indicates excellent conditions. A video, an instructor's guide, and a video guide and training workbook are available to assist with professional development. Yet, in spite of supporting programs carefully looking at environment and its effect on learning, and the ongoing technical assistance provided in many cases, the assessment doesn't support professional development for teachers of young children in a deep or generative way. The two most commented upon items are questions about how many times a day is really necessary for children to wash their hands, and how people are pleased that there is much more artwork (sometimes child-created) at the children's eye level in the classrooms. Shouldn't there be deeper, more context-specific, meaningful questions being asked?

A complicated example in reality shows a program that consistently receives high scores on ECERS evaluations with classrooms that are aesthetically pleasing with interesting and engaging natural materials for the children. However, this doesn't always make for a perfect program for young children. The state-funded program (in the United States) with preschool-aged children is designed based upon the recommendations of Reggio Emilia early childhood programs in Italy. The aesthetics of the classroom are emphasized. Teacher education students come to our class having visited the program for the first time and say, "Oh it is so beautiful and calming. I want to make my house that way." The Reggio Emilia approach pays great attention to the look and feel of the classroom. It is easy to see, from the moment you walk into a Reggio-inspired preschool, why the environment is considered the "third teacher," implying that children learn a vast amount through observing and interacting with the environment. The layout of the physical space in the schools encourages encounters, communication, and relationships.

Yet, in our university classes critical questions are brought up by student teachers. A question I invariably get from the teacher education students is, "Is it okay for the teachers [at this particular program] to be constantly on their cell phones while watching the children on the playground?" Of course it is not; there is a contradiction between the quality of aesthetics and the intentionality of daily care routines here. Of course, this is not a cause-and-effect phenomenon, but all of these aspects of an early care and education program are vitally important and no aspect can be ignored.

Another assessment tool that has become popular nationwide and has been adopted by Head Start and many other programs is the Classroom Assessment Scoring System (CLASS) According to the creators of the Classroom Assessment Scoring System,

> The Classroom Assessment Scoring System™ (CLASS™) is a method for understanding, measuring, and improving teacher-child interactions (Pianta, La Paro, & Hamre, 2008). It includes observational measures of teacher-child interactions and professional development supports to improve these interactions. (Vitello, 2013, p. 2).

Vitello (2013) compiled a brief titled *Dual Language Learners and the CLASS™ Measure: Research and Recommendations* to address many concerns that researchers and practitioners in the field of early childhood had about the assessment, in particular for dual-language learners.

While, of course, teacher-child interaction is of great significance in early learning settings, it is just one piece of a complicated web of interactions. Child-to-child interactions are also of ultimate importance, as is the children's need to experience small-group and large-group social competence. Furthermore, as any early childhood teacher will affirm, focusing on one-on-one child interactions is not something that most teachers are able to do, ethically or practically, for long periods of time, due to the number of children in each setting. Because of the adult-child ratios and budget cuts, as well as having fewer parent volunteers, a teacher's primary responsibility is to the whole group of children in her/his care.

An incident that illustrates a problem with the underlying design and premise of this assessment happened a few years ago. I was introduced to a new faculty member in early childhood at a university when I was working in New York City. She had worked in her graduate program as a lead researcher on Dr. Robert Pianta's project collecting data on aspects of teacher-child interactions in early childhood classrooms. I asked her to tell me about the experience and her resulting thoughts about the development of CLASS. She reported that she was happy that research was finally documenting the importance of human interaction as ultimately one of the most important aspects of conditions for children's learning. She also explained the emphasis on assessing the teacher's interactions with single children. I told her what I was thinking: Of course, everyone would say a teacher's interactions with each child is important, but the National Head Start Association was in negotiations to require all Head Start programs across the country to institute CLASS...and to pay for the professional development for teachers that would be ongoing every year, at great expense. I explained to my new colleague that I was gravely worried about her mentor's new assessment tool for two reasons: (1) In my world of supporting early childhood professionals in programs in financially challenged situations, virtually all teachers must focus on intensely sensitive interactions with every child in their care, not just one, and (2) with Head Start struggling to provide funds for fewer than three of five eligible children. It seemed that the financial burden of the cost of this assessment would make funding matters even worse.

She didn't think the funding issue would be a problem (really?), and she had seen teachers perfect their skills focusing on individual children and then become more skilled at interactions with large groups of children. I asked what she considered a "large" group. "Oh, ten or maybe a few more." And I asked about the complications for teachers who may not speak one of the seven or more home languages represented in her care.

I was on my way to the Henry Street Settlement House's two early childhood centers that morning. I invited the new colleague to join me. Henry Street Settlement Day Care Center cares for children between the ages of 2 and 4. Services available in English, Spanish, and Chinese provide a warm and safe environment, with a stated goal to support and enhance the social, physical, intellectual, creative, and emotional development of young children. Teachers implement the Creative Curriculum, which fosters the development of a positive self-concept and cognitive skills, with a focus on the creative process, integrating music, movement, drama, and arts and crafts. Universal pre-kindergarten is also offered for 4-year-old children at 301 Henry Street. This enriched educational program is designed to prepare children for kindergarten and beyond. Both early childhood programs are licensed by the New York City Department of Health and meet the requirements of all regulatory agencies.

We walked in to see many children in each of the program rooms, and numbers of parents observing and talking with staff. My new friend was a good sport and stayed for the 2-hour time frame that I needed to interact with and observe student teachers. As we left and walked to the subway, her facial expression showed that she was sort of shocked. She said, "You've given me a lot to think about" (Quintero, 2013, n.p.).

Fast-forward a number of years, and yes, CLASS was adopted by National Head Start and many other state-funded programs throughout the country. A group of California-based organizations and individuals who have successfully impacted California's early learning public policies (including child and program assessments, frameworks, curricula, professional development, family engagement, data and research, evaluation, and workforce development) is the Campaign for Quality Early Education (CQEE). Over the past 2 years this group has monitored and raised concerns about the implementation of the early education observation tool CLASS (Classroom Assessment Scoring System) in early care and learning environments where children do not understand or speak English, or are at varying levels of English proficiency (dual-language learners, or DLLs).

The Campaign for Quality Early Education Coalition (Zepeda et al., 2013) wrote a rejoinder to Teachstone's "Dual Language Learners and the Class Measure" to challenge some claims made by Teachstone, stated in Vitello's (2013) brief. The rejoinder states:

> Our primary concerns focus on: 1) the contradictory argument that human behavior is universal while also stating that culture influences how individuals interact in the teaching-learning context; and 2) discussion of research cited to support the utility of the CLASS with DLL (Dual Language Learner) populations which fails to note important aspects of the research that would lead to a more nuanced and qualified set of conclusions with respect to DLL populations. (Zepeda et al., 2013, p. 2)

It is estimated that 36% of all children entering kindergarten in California come from homes where English is not the primary language (Gil & Bardack, 2010). California educates one-third of all dual-language learners in the United States. This is approximately 5.3 million children, or 9–10% of the U.S. school population (Batalova & McHugh, 2010). According to the UCLA Center for Health Public Policy Institute by Children Now, there are 1.6 million, or 57% of California children under the age of 5 who live in a home where a language other than English is spoken (Gil & Bardack, 2010).

It is not just a California issue. Nor is it an issue that has just arisen. In 2003 a Cuban American student teacher in an early childhood master's credential program who was teaching in a bilingual preschool in New Jersey joined one of my university classes. She had been a teacher in that preschool for a number of years. She knew many of the children's families, and she is a Spanish/English bilingual who understands the sociolinguistics of dialectic differences and the importance of vocabulary, register, and altering speech according to context, audience, and intent. And she negotiated this knowledge and her leadership in supporting young children's experiences and opportunities to learn these things. Then came a newly developed bilingual assessment measure developed for Spanish/English bilingual preschoolers. The teacher was required to administer the assessment in a very scripted format. She noticed right away that the Spanish used in the assessment might be more understandable to the children than the English. However, the Spanish used in the assessment was from a different part of the world, where vocabulary, linguistic nuance, and general language use is very different from what was familiar in the Cuban American neighborhood. She came to our university class after the second day of administering the assessment. She was in tears as she told us the story: "They know so much more. They know the concepts and the words in their vernacular. But if they didn't answer exactly as the assessment dictated, I had to mark them as not knowing. It is just wrong" (Quintero, 2006). This takes us full circle back to assessment issues specifically related to home language of the children being assessed.

Learning Story Model from New Zealand: Assessment Tied to Curriculum

Participants in this study and I believe that the New Zealand model of Learning Story assessment is more comprehensive and more appropriate for participation among teachers, children, and parents—including culture and language—and therefore more authentic. Learning Stories were developed in New Zealand by Margaret Carr and her colleagues (2001). They are "a particular form of documented and structured observations that use a narrative form of documentation of the strengths of children and their progression of activities. There is an underlying agenda of protecting and developing children's identities as learners in accordance with the national early childhood curriculum" (Carr, 2001, p. 29). *Te Whāriki*, New Zealand's national bicultural, bilingual (English and Maori) curriculum for early years, was developed by early childhood professionals in New Zealand and supported at the national level. It is a curriculum founded on the following aspirations for children:

> ...to grow up as competent and confident learners and communicators, healthy in mind, body and spirit, secure in their sense of belonging and in the knowledge that they make a valued contribution to society. (New Zealand Ministry of Education, 2010)

The Learning Stories approach to assessment has been praised by a number of writers. For example, Smith (2003, p. 12), states: "Learning Stories seem to have extraordinary power to excite and energise teachers, parents and children. Parents have become much more interested in and convinced of the extraordinary learning achievements of children in their early childhood centres." Some early childhood teachers have described the value of Learning Stories for facilitating understandings of literacy (Hatherly, 2006) and for promoting communication between teachers, children, and families (Ramsey, Sturm, Breen, Lee, & Carr, 2007). Carr's own research provides case-study evidence to support the value of Learning Stories for children and teachers (Carr, 2001). However, there is not total agreement about the usefulness or importance of such assessments. One critic, Blaiklock (2008), says "While

Learning Stories have the potential to capture important aspects of children's experiences in centres, there are questions about whether they are an effective and practical means of assessing the richness of children's learning in a diverse range of early childhood contexts" (p. 78).

Learning Stories are a type of assessment that uses qualitative research techniques. Carr (1999, cited in Smith, 2003, p. 11) states that the narrative-based Learning Stories can be seen as a form of action research. This methodology requires strategies such as peer debriefing, prolonged engagement and persistent observation, and member checks (Morse, Barrett, Mayan, Olson, & Spiers, 2002).

While Blaiklock (2008) believes that it is "unrealistic to expect early childhood educators to carry out assessment with the same rigor and verification procedures that are required in qualitative research" (p. 79), Carr (2001) proposed four major ways to achieve accountability in relation to Learning Stories:

1. "Keeping the data transparent" (e.g., by providing observation information, in the form of stories, that is accessible).
2. "Ensuring that a range of interpreters have their say" (e.g., by having a number of staff discuss the interpretation of a Learning Story).
3. "Refining the constructs as they appear locally" (e.g., by staff agreeing on how children exhibit particular behaviours that indicate particular dispositions).
4. "Being clear about the connection between the learner and the environment" (e.g., by seeing that learning occurs within a socio-cultural setting). (pp. 183–184)

Context of Storying Learning Assessment in Our Study

For the purpose of our adaptation of the Learning Story model, we have labeled our version of this type of assessment "Storying Learning." We wanted to acknowledge the leadership of the New Zealand colleagues in the field while being transparent about our adaptation of their model. So, to reiterate, at the same time that university students are beginning their study of collaborative (with children) curriculum development and working in their student teaching placements, they are also taking a concurrent assessment class along with the curriculum class. The textbook for the assessment class is *Learning Stories: Constructing Learner Identities in Early Education* by Carr and Lee (2012). The professors and students also relied heavily on the New Zealand Ministry of Education website about early childhood assessment and development (2010).

The university assessment class uses problem-posing (based on critical theory), similar to that used in the curriculum class (explained in Chapter 2), to support students' understanding and use of the information in the curriculum as they grapple with issues of assessment. This method nourishes an integrated curriculum that supports young children's meaningful learning (Quintero, 2009; Quintero & Rummel, 1995). To reiterate, the problem-posing method is comprised of several components. These are: *listening, dialogue,* and *action.* In this method, participants:

- listen to their own histories through reflective writing and sharing of participants' stories, and gather new information in the form of mini-lectures, expert presentations, or scholarly research and academic information;
- dialogue about information that was shared and presented during the listening activities; discuss issues of power that have shaped their identities and current families, schools, and communities contexts; and make connections to the situations of the children and families they work with, using personal and historical information; and
- collaborate on various curricular activities that encourage and support action or transformation on the part of children, families, and educators.

For example, in the listening section of one assessment class, the students were asked to review the field notes in their journals and identify a child or a small group of children that they had been focused on, noting patterns in the day-to-day experiences of the children. In the dialogue section, the students shared their data about the children with a partner. Then in the action section, they participated in jigsaw activity about a certain topic such as learning dispositions in the Carr and Lee (2012) text. Then, they were asked to refer to the New Zealand Ministry of Education website and, using the learning story of one toddler, Daniel, as a guide, review their own journal notes about children they were working with and make an outline of a storying learning narrative about literacy learning on chart paper. They then shared their thoughts with the whole class. The structure of the storying learning narratives in these examples was a simple narrative description that answered the following questions:

(1) What's happening?
(2) What aspect of child input does this assessment exemplify?
(3) How might this documented assessment contribute to developing competence with identified goals and standards?
(4) What might this assessment tell us about your specific integrated curriculum and the children's responses in this setting?
(5) What's next?

In an action homework assignment given toward the end of the semester of the combined curriculum and assessment class, students are assigned activities such as the ones described below, in which they continue practicing going into more depth with the curriculum work and understanding the curriculum and assessment connections. The activities include:

- Look at your own activity/experience plans for your Integrated Curriculum and write about new learning, creativity, excitement, or constructed knowledge that children will potentially experience. Your cooperating teachers have supported children during lots of conceptual learning experiences to date. Your work should not repeat that learning but build upon it, and always be based on your observations of the children.
- Choose a learning story handout as a model, and write a Storying Learning narrative about a child doing her/his work.
- Read Chapter 5 in Carr & Lee, and write a rough draft of Storying Learning Assessment about a young child you currently work with.

An example of student rough-draft Storying Learning assessment comes from the case study excerpts of the student teacher we call Celeste:

Today, during my smoothie making lesson activity for the toddler group, I was sitting with the children at the rectangle table. They were all very attentive because this activity was different for them and they hadn't done it before. There is one child, Ben, who usually doesn't participate in group time, and a teacher does an individual activity with him while the other children are in groups with other teachers. He mostly speaks Spanish but doesn't have a big vocabulary and is going to speech therapy. Today, he went with the teacher but he slowly got closer to our group and wanted to see what we were doing. I think the blender caught his attention because he was staring at it. I thought it would be a great activity for him as he could participate, and I thought having him be the child who turns on the blender would be perfect for him because he likes to make a lot of noise and is very active. I assigned an ingredient of the smoothie to each child and assigned turning on and off the blender to Ben.

Ben is usually very impatient and doesn't sit for long, but he was different during this lesson. He waited very patiently as the children measured out their ingredient and added it to the blender he was holding. I asked them what they thought was going to happen to all the ingredients when Ben turned on the blender. Ben said "smoothie." When everyone added their ingredient, I helped him put the blender in the base and he turned it on. He was amazed and pointed to the blender and said, "Smoothie!" I asked him in Spanish what he saw and he said, "se esta mezclando" (it is mixing). He kept telling me things in Spanish like that he wanted to drink the smoothie and that the blender was loud.

As a result of participating in this activity, I learned that Ben is able to express himself and use words when he does things that are interesting to him and when he is spoken to or is speaking in his home language. The teachers in the classroom are not able to get him to talk much or participate in activities. Their not knowing Spanish has a lot to do with it because he can't understand them. I learned that he has a larger vocabulary than the teachers think, because he was communicating with me in sentences, which he doesn't do with the teachers. I also learned that he can work well with others. Usually, he doesn't participate in group activities because the teachers think he can't, and that he needs one-on-one attention. However, he worked very well with his peers at my activity. I helped him throughout my activity in being patient and cooperating with his peers. I think Ben is capable of working well with his peers and using language more. He needs the guidance of a bilingual adult to help him through this, though.

Ben is not one of the children whom I planned the lesson for that like to pretend cook a lot. He really enjoys running and playing with trains. However, because of other children's input I was able to give this experience to Ben. I also learned a lot about Ben by doing this lesson. My standards were reflected when the children interacted easily with each other in this shared activity where each child was assigned an ingredient and they saw each other measure and add it to the blender. I had a large poster with the recipe for our smoothie and we kept referring back to it and reading the numbers to see how much we needed of each ingredient. They also followed instructions that were a one- or two-step sequence by counting the ingredients, measuring, and pouring into blender. (Quintero, 2013, n.p.)

Storying Learning Example From *The Rag Coat* Lesson Plan

Finally, an assessment from Ana, who created the lessons about weather changes mentioned in Chapter 3 and earlier in this chapter.

Introduction:

1. **What's happening here?**

After [I have read] *The Rag Coat* to the morning class as a large group, Child C finds a spot at the blue table to participate in the art portion of the lesson. He carefully picks out scraps of fabric to glue on his paper person. As he is gluing the scraps on his person, he engages in self talk by narrating what he is doing. I recorded Child C saying, "I am putting a coat on my person so he could stay warm like the girl in the story."

Interpretation:

2. **What have you learned about this child's development and learning as a result of participating in your activity?**

I have learned that Child C is able to connect the events in the anchor text to the art activity. The literature shared during our large group time was about a girl who wishes to go to school, but is worried because she does not have a coat for the winter. The mothers in her village make her a coat to stay warm. Child C quickly caught on to this message and theme of kindness and selflessness when he responded about his artwork.

3. **What's next for your child?**

Seeing that Child C was interested in the collage activity, I will incorporate this into more lessons. Also, Child C showed an interest in expressing kindness to others, as he made additional comments about making clothes for his friends. With this evidence, I may carry the theme of kindness in future discussions and find other texts that incorporate this theme.

Conclusion:

4. What aspects of child input are reflected in this learning story?

The children in the morning class gave me the idea for this lesson based on their comments about the changing weather and the fact that they now have to wear long sleeves and big jackets. Particularly, Child C gave constant input on the new jacket that his mom bought him for the snow and cold weather.

5. What evidence of your standards is reflected?

Child C quickly learned the theme of the story and lesson. In his artwork and comments on making a coat so his person can stay warm, Child C reflected the California Preschool Learning Foundations regarding empathy, caring, and social and emotional understanding. These standards specify that children over 60 months of age should begin to comprehend the mental and psychological reasons people act as they do, and how they contribute to differences between people. In addition, the standard defining empathy and caring in regard to preschool-age children states that they should be able to respond to another's distress and needs with sympathetic caring, and are more likely to assist. Child C's actions in the making of his art project and during the reading of the text show these skills' emerging development.

6. If possible, include parent's voice.

Child C gave constant input on the new jacket that his mom bought him for the snow and cold weather. His mom is an avid volunteer for the school and works part-time for the school library. She frequently comes to check on him. During the day of this lesson, Child C's mom came in after he finished his art project. Child C was excited to share that he dressed up his person so he could be warm. I walked over to explain the activity and Child C made it known that he had a really cool new jacket. I asked if he could wear it to school, but his mom explained it was a little too heavy for the weather considering it was a snow jacket. Child C's family often visits relatives who experience snowy weather. This showed me that Child C is very familiar with extreme cold winter climates, which may be why he was so empathetic to the young girl in the story who did not have a coat. (Quintero, 2013, n.p.)

What Does One Professional Organization Say?

The National Association for the Education of Young Children (NAEYC) and the National Association of Early Childhood Specialists in the State Departments of Education (NAECS/SDE) have made recommendations about assessments for children birth to age 8. A joint position statement reads, "Make ethical, appropriate, valid and reliable assessments a central part of all early childhood programs" (National Association for the Education of Young Children, 2003). Effective assessment is dependent on many conditions. NAEYC indicators of effectiveness include:

- Ethical principles guide assessment practices.
- Assessment instruments are used for their intended purposes.
- Assessments are appropriate for ages and other characteristics (cultures, home languages, socioeconomic status, abilities and disabilities) of children being assessed.
- Assessment instruments are in compliance with professional criteria for quality.
- What is assessed is developmentally and educationally significant.
- Assessment evidence is used to understand and improve learning. (National Association for the Education of Young Children, 2003)

However, these points only hint at the intricate issues involved in assessment of programs for young children and assessment of the children's experiences and learning. What about Juan, Melina, the girls upset about the slippers whose teacher doesn't talk to them in their home language, and Fernando, who wants to play "writing homework" rather than sitting still on the carpet listening to his teacher? There are positive and wonderful complexities about the children and their situations. And there are distressing aspects about some of the situations. Are we being insincere, or just not thinking as we and our professional organizations make grand statements about ethics, development, and quality of programming, when we don't acknowledge the day-to-day living situations of the children and their families?

Assessment is a complex topic in every situation. In the field of early care and education, the dilemmas of authenticity, ethics, efficacy, and consistency are mind-boggling. As discussed in Chapter 1, many researchers and policy makers acknowledge that for years, the political winds have influenced assessment decisions based upon faulty research. Equally complicated is the fact that research that documents the dramatic influence early childhood education can have on young children is based on programs that meet certain "quality indicators" (Matthews, 2013). More to come in Chapter 5. *Quality* is a subjective term that is often considered with an objective construct. Chapter 5 brings this point clearly to the forefront.

References

Batalova, J., & McHugh, M. (2010) Number and Growth of Students in U.S. Schools in Need of English Instruction. (Washington, DC: Migration Policy Institute. Retrieved from http://www.migrationinformation.org/ellinfo/FactSheet_ELL1.pdf

Blaiklock, K. E. (2008). A critique of the use of learning stories to assess the learning dispositions of young children. *New Zealand Research in Early Childhood Education, 11,* 77–87.

Bloch, M. N. (2014). Interrogating *Reconceptualizing Early Care and Education* (RECE)—20 years along. In M. N. Bloch, B. B. Swadener, & G. S. Cannella (Eds.), *Reconceptualizing early childhood care and education: A reader* (pp. 19–31). New York: Peter Lang.

Carr, M. (2001). *Assessment in early childhood settings: Learning stories.* Thousand Oaks, CA: Sage.

Carr, M. (1999). Being a Learner: Five Learning Dispositions for Early Childhood. *Early Childhood Practice,* Waikato, New Zealand: The University of Waikato.

Carr, M., Duncan, J., Lee, W., Jones, C., Marshall, K., & Smith, A. (2009). *Learning in the making: Disposition and design in early education.* Rotterdam, Netherlands: Sense Publishing.

Carr, M., & Lee, W. (2012). *Learning stories: Constructing learner identities in early education.* New York: Sage.

Gil, L., & Bardack, S. (2010). *Common assumptions vs. the evidence: English language learners in the United States. A reference guide.* Washington, DC: American Institutes for Research. Retrieved from http://www.air.org/files/ELL_Assumptions_and_Evidence.pdf

Hatherly, A. (2006). The stories we share: Using narrative assessment to build communities of literacy participants in early childhood centres. *Australian Journal of Early Childhood, 31*(1), 27–34.

Matthews, D. (2013, February 14). James Heckman: In early childhood education, "Quality really matters." *Washington Post.* Retrieved from http://www.washingtonpost.com/blogs/wonkblog/wp/2013/02/14/james-heckman-in-early-childhood-education-quality-really-matters/

Morse, J. M., Barrett, M., Mayan, M., Olson, K., & Spiers, J. (2002). Verification strategies for establishing reliability and validity in qualitative research. *International Journal of Qualitative Methods*, *1*(2), 13–22.

National Association for the Education of Young Children. (2003). *Early childhood curriculum assessment and program evaluation*. Retrieved from https://www.naeyc.org/files/naeyc/file/positions/pscape.pdf

New Zealand Ministry of Education. (2010). *Part A: ECE Educate*. Retrieved from http://www.educate.ece.govt.nz/learning/curriculumAndLearning/TeWhariki/PartA.aspx

Pacini-Ketchabaw, V. (Ed.). (2010). *Flows, rhythms, and intensities of early childhood education curriculum*. New York: Peter Lang.

Quintero, E. (2006). Research journal. unpublished manuscript.

Quintero, E. P. (2009). *Artful story: Critical literacy in early childhood curriculum*. New York: Peter Lang.

Quintero, E. P. (2013). Research journal (unpublished manuscript).

Quintero, Elizabeth P., & Rummel, Mary K. (1995). Voice unaltered: Marginalized young writers speak. In Swadener, E. B. & Lubeck, S. (Eds.), *Children and families at promise: The social construction of risk* (pp. 97–117). New York, NY: State University of New York.

Ramsey, K., Sturm, J., Breen, J., Lee, W., & Carr, M. (2007). Weaving ICTs into *Te Whāriki* at Roskill South Kindergarten. In A. Meade (Ed.), *Cresting the waves: Innovation in early childhood education* (pp. 29–35). Wellington: NZCER Press.

Ritchie, J., & Rau, C. (2009). Ma wai nga hua? "Participation" in early childhood in Aotearoa/New Zealand. *International Critical Childhood Policy Studies*, *2*(1), 93–108.

Smith, A. B. (2003, July). *Te Whāriki: Diversity or standardisation? Innovative aspects of the New Zealand early childhood curriculum*. Paper presented at Education in the Early Years: International Developments and Implications for Germany, Munich, Germany.

Taylor, A. (2013). *Reconfiguring the natures of childhood*. London: Routledge, Chapman & Hall.

Vitello, Virginia E. (2013). *Dual language learners and the CLASS measure: Research and recommendations*. Charlottesville, VA: Teachstone Training.

Zepeda, M., Cline, Z., Oh, J., Matera, C., Espinosa, L., Lopez, L., … Kurtz, D. (2013). *Rejoinder to Teachstone's "Dual Language Learners and the CLASS Measure."* Los Angeles: Campaign for Quality Early Education. Retrieved from http://www.afabc.org/What-we-do/Education/Early-Care---Education/CQEE-Coalition-1.aspx

· 5 ·

EARLY CHILDHOOD ISSUES:
AN UNDERSTATEMENT

Curriculum, Assessment, Young Children:
Overlapping Complexities

In the midst of the complex work involved with teacher education, and honing in on curriculum and assessment, it becomes clearer than ever that in early childhood, the issues which must be considered are tangles of webs that are sometimes overlapping and always influencing each other in one way or many ways. We will be guided through these interconnected and complicated issues by our children guides—some of the children who have been discussed throughout this book by way of case study excerpts. Also, the case study excerpts by student teachers will help illustrate some of the related issues in their particular contexts. Both the children and the student teachers will be doing their jobs as bricoleurs as they help illuminate findings about the issues that in a myriad of ways affect both curriculum and assessment.

My trajectory of work, learning, passion, and commitment have led me to do what I do. And finally, the findings of this study have insisted that I pay attention to these issues in the webs of interconnectivity. I was a teaching assistant and then a teacher working with children and families from multiple histories with multiple linguistic backgrounds and a wealth of strengths and unmet needs. I learned a little about working in classrooms, a lot about children and their families, and how difficult our work could be. I thought I learned about theory and practice. But I always knew there would definitely be more to learn with each situation and each new group of children.

So, in the process of addressing these issues in my work, I collected ideas, assumptions, and hypotheses about multilingual children's roots of literacy and the ways their parents and early teachers could support them. Shortly after completing my dissertation on literacy development in bilingual preschoolers, I had the opportunity to design an intergenerational family literacy program that became Project FIEL in El Paso, Texas (federally funded by the Office of Bilingual Education and Minority Languages Affairs as a demonstration project). I was confident about the strength of the child/parent relationship and I knew that the innate enthusiasm of every child to learn and flourish in a meaningful social context would make a literacy class in which parents studied alongside their children dynamic and interesting. I felt certain that the family bond and the opportunity to engage in appropriately flexible activities would make it possible to transcend difficulties such as different patterns of language dominance, different literacy abilities, and different learning needs.

My career journey soon took me to working in bilingual family literacy with Hmong and Somali families in Duluth, Minnesota. I learned about context from Ms. Moua who had grown up in the refugee camps in Thailand; she spoke seven languages and had never had the opportunity to study math. I learned about cultural complexity and more about history when Somali families joined the family literacy discussions. Later, while at NYU, with groups of education and culture and communication students studying in London with the United Nations High Commissioner for Refugees providing programs for asylum seekers, we learned about supporting migrating families internationally.

Now programs in higher education in the United States that systematically educate professionals to serve children and families are often beholden to funders of both programs and research. Often, conflicting ideas and misconceptions about issues such as "quality" are evident among the funders, the academic programs, and publicly and privately funded early care and education programs in the early childhood field used as field placement sites. I say misconceptions because as early childhood grows and expands as a field, the issues become more complex. To grossly oversimplify, it has occurred to me that no matter what dramatic changes we promote regarding how we provide curriculum and conduct assessments with creative, responsive, intelligent, and critical teachers, none of us operates in a vacuum. Yes, even when findings are unexpected, they must be attended to.

Funding for early childhood programs depends upon assumptions and values of the country where the program is located. Often, funding depends upon measures of "quality" that purport to be objective measures, when in fact, quality represents subjective priorities defined by policy makers, politicians, and in many places in the United States, business CEOs who have no information about, or experience with, young children. While participants and I during this study were diligently thinking about and addressing curriculum and assessment, we collected findings with themes that screamed at us to pay attention as they relate to curriculum, assessment, and broader contexts of children and their families. So what do we collectively, internationally, know about children's growth, experience, and support? Is our knowledge building upon formerly developed theoretical information and new information? Does some of the new information conflict with the old? What can be done to bring new research, assumptions, and perspectives into our work?

Child Development, Theories, and Contexts

Child development is the discipline that is commonly believed to offer a systematic, objective, and scientific study of childhood. Penn (2014) reminds us that there are problems in understanding and interpreting the everyday world of children (or anyone else). These problems can be summarized as universality versus particularity, continuity versus discontinuity, objectivity versus subjectivity, competing disciplinary frameworks, and translating theory into practice. We learn from recent work by Katherine Nelson (2009) that

> Meaning is in the mind and the brain; it is also in the body that recognizes familiar things and places. Meaning comes to reside in the child, but it also resides in the social world, in the affect-laden interactions with caretakers and others, in the symbols and artifacts of the culture, in the language spoken around the child. (p. 10)

Nelson (2009) rejects the notion that development is, and the study of development should be, objective. She says, "The major breakthrough in human development, the one I believe finally made us different from all other animals, was the ability to share subjective meanings" (p. 10).

As outrageous as it may sound to generations of early childhood professionals who have studied and applied principles of child development as the

discipline is in Western Europe and the United States, we must ask some difficult questions. Penn (2014) urges us to consider whether or not it is possible,
through systematic observation and experimentation, to identify universal,
age-related traits that all children in all contexts have in common, and use
these as the basis for developing a science of childhood.

Foundational Theories in Early Childhood

The foundational theories in early childhood are well known and have been
important to our young and growing field of study. Yet, as the theories relate
to children and contexts in our current world, it is impossible not to acknowledge that they reflect a narrow conception of children.

> Piaget wrote in the chaotic aftermath of two world wars, when it seemed important
> to argue that human beings were essentially rational creatures, capable of abstract
> logical thought, even if the recent experiences of mankind were a shock horror story.
> (Penn, 2014, p. 45)

In the United Kingdom and other Western contexts, Piaget's ideas "chimed
in with nursery school traditions of play. Children had always been allowed to
play in nursery school. Piaget provided a theoretical legitimation of 'learning
through play'" (Penn, 2014, p. 46). Piaget's work inspired many psychologists to test out his theories. Piaget's contributions became famously used and
quoted throughout the world in spite of his lack of emphasis on social and
cultural influences. His focus was clearly on epistemology, or how things come
to be known.

This brings us back to the story of Fernando, introduced in Chapter 3. Fernando was in a state-funded preschool in Southern California. While a large
percentage of the children are Spanish-speaking and just learning English for
the first time, the school does not promote support of home language except
in emergencies or when speaking with parents. The student teacher working
with Fernando, Pam, herself a bilingual California native, was in a sensitive
position of trying to almost subversively support the 4-year-olds' use of their
home languages. She wrote a lengthy journal report about Fernando, the situation, and his potential. The vignette is repeated here as it points to a child
who is developing in complex ways in spite of the misconceptions of many of
his teachers.

I am assigned to sit with 4-year-old Fernando who is unable to sit down on the rug during literacy time. Since he is unable to control his behavior, and sit quietly cross-ing his legs (that all children are requested to do) Fernando is told to sit in a chair.

Fernando shows interest in my notebook as soon as he notices I am writing notes. He wants to write his name. "Fernando, you may write your name as soon as we go out and play. Let's listen to Teacher right now."

"Yo escribo mi nombre?" (Do I write my name?), he asks me in Spanish. "Si, despues que salgamos a jugar afuera" (Yes, after we go to play outside), I answer him back in Spanish. "Ok, Teacher. Gracias." He turns to listen to his other teacher.

As soon as we are outside during play time, Fernando runs up to me, "Teacher Pam, yo hago homework" (Teacher Pam, I do homework). "You do your homework?" I ask. "No! Tu homework!" (No, your homework!). He wants to do my homework. I give him my notepad, unsure what he means. He begins writing. He writes, then looks up, around, then writes some more. (Quintero, 2013, n.p.)

She then reflects on what she has learned about the child and his learning context, and about herself as a professional:

My new friend, Fernando, cannot manage to sit still with his peers, but he'd been observing me and noticed I take notes. It seems that our friendship and what he's noticed me doing (writing) have become important to him, and he can communicate it all with me in his home language. (Quintero, 2013, n.p.)

In other words, when a social relationship develops—with an adult who speaks his home language with him—and the child keenly observes his new friend involved in an activity that is important to her (taking notes), he shows focused interest and potential.

Earlier, in Chapter 1, we were introduced to Melina. She was 4 years of age and was very social and enjoyed having conversations with her teacher. Melina invited the student teacher to play with her. They were working (play-ing) with geometric shapes at the manipulatives table. Their conversation revealed through Melina's story that she has a vivid image of her hometown in Mexico, her grandpa's ranch, and the differences between types of animals, and she is able to recreate her images through objects to tell her story (Quin-tero, 2014). Will this child's experiences in school give her opportunities to use and enhance her sophisticated knowledge that is so closely tied to the meaning of family and place?

Yoshikawa et al. (2013) compiled current research relating to the evidence base for quality early childhood programs for all children. Yet, it is still important to ask, how was it decided what "evidence" would be included in this "evidence base" (Dahlberg, Moss, & Pence, 2013)? And even with the expansive list of collaborators on Yoshikawa's research compilation, is their collective view of "evidence" meaningful for and reflective of families in our communities across the country and the world (Dahlberg et al., 2013)?

Vygotsky's ideas brought in many areas of psychology—for instance, ideas about communities of practice and activity theory. Bruner has reflected in intelligent ways the changes in theorizing about child development. "He has moved from Piaget, through Vygotsky and Chomsky, to a view that to learn is to create meanings from the stream of events and activities within one's own society. He has become interested in narrative and the construction of identity" (Penn, 2014, p. 49).

We will be introduced to several children in Chapter 8 who, through their symbolic, pretend play, are exhibiting a complex combination of experimenting with fantasy versus reality, learning to negotiate caring, empathetic relationships with peers, and confirming their own and their friends' identities. Are their abilities and creations respected as evidence?

Experiences surrounding narrative and identity are starkly relevant to the large population of indigenous people from Oaxaca, Mexico, the Mixtecs, now living and working in California. One student teacher working in a program, Fran, wrote in her journal:

> There is one 4-year-old girl that I noticed was always quiet, never responds to a "good morning" or to a "What are you drawing?" in English or Spanish. She always smiles and nods. I finally asked the teacher if she ever talks when I'm not around. I found out that her home language is Mixteco! At home she hears one language, then at school two other languages. I think that her looking at us when we talk to her is a good sign. At least I know the information is sinking in. I hope.
>
> Songs are sung in both English and Spanish. Pamphlets, brochures, and flyers are also bilingual. Everyone that works there speaks both English and Spanish. The teachers sit with parents to discuss child progress. As far them helping Mixteco speakers, I haven't seen anything. (Quintero, 2013, n.p.)

Many of our students work in programs where there are numbers of children and families from the Mixtec community. Some issues regarding the context of this community of people living in the United States are discussed in Chapter 1. In spite of very difficult barriers, some Mixtec parents whom our student

teachers in early childhood got to know had knowledge and passionate determination about what they want for their children. The findings and responses
documented that 99% preferred "Bilingual English and Spanish and another
language if possible" in early and general education for their children. These
wishes were repeated over and over as parents explained the stress of raising
children who often feel shame associated with their culture (Quintero, 2012).

Katherine Nelson (2009) points to the now substantial body of evidence
that has arisen from focusing on the "real world" of language learning, of individual children in their homes. She documents "a bottom-up, pragmatic, expe-
rience-dependent, bio-social-cultural developmental system of knowing" (p. x).
She explains that this evidence implies different views of evolution, representation, conceptual development, and the role of language in cognitive development. Of course. The bricoleur children, working with a student teacher, give us
strong reason to consider this different approach to development.

One student teacher, Leila, who had been studying Spanish but was not
yet bilingual, wrote of her worries about her lack of language knowledge:

> Last semester I feared that I wouldn't be able to teach children who shared a different
> primary language than I did. I shared this concern with one of my professors, and
> she told me that language should not get in the way of my teaching. She said that
> if I listened to the children and planned well for them, the language wouldn't be a
> problem and that the materials would create the language. I didn't understand this
> at all. Probably because of teaching practices I've seen before where teachers talk a
> LOT and children talk a little. What I ended up learning was how true the things my
> professor had told me were. The scariest lesson plan I implemented was a long piece
> of butcher paper rolled out across a wall with the words "Family Wall" and "la pared
> de la familia" written across the top and crayons on the ground below. Amazingly,
> and much to my surprise, the conversation came. The children spoke to one another
> about their work. They spoke to me about their work. They spoke to other teachers
> about their work. I learned more about the few children that I saw working over 3
> days than I had about them over the course of a semester. I think that was the point
> that I knew that I needed to understand research better than I did because I wanted
> to know what to do with some of the amazing things I was learning about children.
> (Quintero, 2013, n.p.)

Negotiating Shared Meanings Through Language and Place

Penn (2014) explains Nelson's claim that even though young infants', toddlers', and preschoolers' minds are private, subjective spaces, the meanings

absorbed are "socially shared, and meaning sharing is the process by which development proceeds...this is not to rule out objectivity or generalization, but instead points to the immense subtlety of research and understanding" (p. 66). Leila, with the help of the bricoleur children, uncovered some of the immense subtlety of understanding.

The student teacher Leila isn't "just talking" in her journal; she is digesting new information she is learning from the children and learning about herself. Above, she mentioned the "Family Wall," which was an initial activity that would become a series of activities she titled, "Neighborhood Maps." Following is an excerpt from her research journal where she begins to develop the rationale for the activities she is planning and some of the specifics to be addressed.

Through the series of activities available, children will be given the opportunity to understand differences among people as well as similarities. Children will have opportunities to learn about themselves and their peers, they will be exposed to print concepts through literature, they will experience ideas about both home communities and global communities, they will be exposed to number sense concepts, and they will have the opportunity to express themselves in the language they feel most comfortable using. These activities support my theoretical framework in the respects of the importance of bilingual education and the value of it for children, that play is children's work, the development of multicultural and adaptive curricula, and an emphasis on families and community.

Extension home: Before bringing the map into the classroom, send home a note with families asking where they are from, where their parents are from, where the majority of their family still lives.

1. Once all of the information is collected and posted on the map in the classroom, I will talk to children during welcome about the information that was collected. I will let them know that anyone interested can help work on the map at outdoor playtime. The map will be composed of the main centers or areas that our children are from pre-constructed by the teacher. (In this case it was a map of California and Mexico).

2. I will provide stickers to plot points, yarn to connect points, markers, paper, scissors, pens, and pencils. Near the map, I will provide a book box with books about geography and different world cultures.

3. I will review the map and different locations with the children each day. Keep this up as a source of continuing learning about geography.

4.   After the map has been up for a couple of days, present a drawing activity to the children to draw a neighborhood map. I will ask them if they know their way to school from their house, where the bakery is in location to school or home, where they play outside, etc.

*This activity could be used with older children by including more mathematics in the activity, for example by measuring distances from location to location on the map using the scale provided. (Quintero, 2013, n.p.)

Leila went on to explain:

Suela approached me while some children were looking at books and she asked me if she could write on the map. The map had just been introduced into the environment that day. I hadn't intended for it to be written on that day, but I agreed with Suela and agreed she could begin writing on the map. I noticed that she began making shapes that looked like a backward C. I scooted closer, and I heard her quietly whisper, A. I looked, and she had just written a perfect capital A. Soon, Suela moved to the Family Wall and continued to write the same letter shapes and then began drawing. When it seemed she was finishing her drawing I asked her what she made. She said, "Un rainbow." I said, "Hmm…a rainbow on the family wall." She said, "Si, un rainbow es una familia."

Leila continued,

I am so glad I agreed about her writing on the wall. Otherwise, I wouldn't have seen the progression of her writing skills. Also, Suela seems to be able to think in abstract concepts in regards to her rainbow drawing and the idea that a rainbow, too, is a family. She is showing confidence and pride in her work. I will continue to provide Suela with opportunities to write and support her learning in regards to her writing skills. Talk more with her about her writing and possibly introduce books like *Chicka Chicka Boom Boom* to increase her literacy and enjoyment of letters and writing. In regards to Suela's drawing, I will continue to stay open-minded about her learning and look at her understanding of abstract concepts and help foster and encourage those ideas as well as discuss with her more to understand her thinking. (Quintero, 2013, n.p.)

Leila explains a few other children's responses to activities that she provided for the children in her research journal:

Julia and Kate are sitting with Rogelio and me while we make neighborhood maps. We began making our maps with school as our center and branching out from there. After determining how to describe far and near (driving versus walking), we added more things to our maps like: home, the grocery store, the beach, and the park. Julia and Kate began arguing when we were discussing where the beach should go on their maps. I prompted by asking, "Do we drive to the beach or do we walk there?" Both girls agreed that we walk there, however Julia argued that "Es un camino largo!" (It is a long road.) Kate said, "No, es muy corto" (No, it's very short). I told them that it could be either, depending on where they are walking from. They drew on their maps according to their own belief about where the beach was located. All of the children then chose to glue their maps onto the large map of California and Mexico.

Julia and Kate are exploring the idea of distance and how it seems to be a relative matter. Although most distances and means of transportation were agreed upon, some were not. I was excited when I saw the children post their maps with the larger maps. They seemed to be grasping the concept of geography, and looking at where things are even if they are a different perspective.

Next it would be interesting to look at physical addresses to assess actual distance for the girls. It would put their learning into a more personal perspective as well. We could develop a large-scale neighborhood map for the classroom and identify where all of the children live in relation to school. These girls might be interested in learning different types of measurement such as city blocks and miles to a destination. It might be fun to bring in a computer and show the girls Google Earth to show the satellite image of our neighborhood. (Quintero, 2013, n.p.)

Twenty-First-Century Contexts and Rethinking Theoretical Foundations

Considering the vast diversity of family histories, geopolitical realities, and living conditions around the world, we must ask whether knowing about "ages and stages of development" illuminates what experiences people have during childhood. Do you remember the story of Juan from Chapter 1? After a couple of weeks of Juan doing all his play and other activities outdoors, the teachers began to bring the learning center activities back indoors, gradually—one each day. After a few weeks of this "change" back to an indoor classroom, Juan began to interact with his friends and teachers inside the classroom in appropriate ways.

At a home visit with his family in October, the site supervisor learned some clues about the mystery of the child's interactions and participation. Juan's mother explained that she and her husband and two children lived in the tiny one-room apartment with two other families. It was clear that when at home, Juan had no opportunity to look outdoors, or play outdoors, and only a few feet of space to play indoors (Quintero, 2014). This situation would not reflect well or accurately through an "ages and stages" evaluation. Scientific theory attempts to be more empirical and logical in exploring phenomena, but it is impossible to comprehensively explain all events in Juan's situation. Thankfully for the child, his parents and teachers were developing a sort of folk theory to think about ways to support Juan's learning and comfort.

In our qualitative study discussed in this book, it is explicitly clear that our intentions and our curriculum and assessment work are framed by critical theory. This perspective is seen in certain venues of education work around the world. It is more often used in work with adults and language acquisition programs. Postmodern theory, however, as Penn (2014) acknowledges,

> is relatively strong in its critiques of classroom and practice and has drawn valuable attention to those who have been marginalized....But none of these initiatives offers a coherent critique of a failing system of early childhood education and care, where not enough money is being spent to ensure a fair service for all children. (p. 31)

Many of us who think about and use critical theory acknowledge this tragedy. It seems we must become more active in sharing the voices of children and families that much of the quantitative statistics miss. With encouragement to live the aspect of critical theory that uses multiple sources of knowledge, students can push the boundaries of what comprises a foundational approach to learning in early childhood. Through their case studies of their own process of becoming and using the three tenets of critical theory of participation, multiple sources of knowledge including family history and experiences, and transformative action, the student teacher participants in this study have shown that they are full of potential.

A student teacher mentioned previously, Fran, also participated in an independent study that developed as an offshoot of her curriculum and assessment study. Fran was interested in the work of Gloria Anzaldúa and became familiar with a theory she developed and called "conocimiento theory." Conocimiento, for Anzaldúa, is

> an overarching theory of consciousness ... all the dimensions of life, both inner—mental, emotional, instinctive, imaginal, spiritual, bodily realms—and outer—social, political, lived experiences ... the awareness of facultad that sees through all human acts, whether of the individual mind and spirit or of the collective, social body. (Hérnandez-Ávila & Anzaldúa, 2000, p. 177–178)

Fran was a senior early childhood studies student teacher and was also working with migrant youth from Mixtec backgrounds (from Oaxaca, Mexico) in an urban high school in Southern California. A segment of a conversation between Fran Martinez and a high school student she tutors hints at the need for a theoretical approach such as conocimiento according to Anzaldúa. This is a way to view and support the strengths and challenges of youth in migrant situations. Fran noted in her journal:

> A young tenth grader approached me asking about my own living situations. "Maestra, usted vive sola?" (Teacher, do you live alone?), she said. I went on to say I had a roommate, then I had to explain what a roommate was, and that I take care of my personal things.

> She asked if I missed my family, but specifically, she asked if I missed my mother. At the moment this wasn't awkward; later I made the connection. A while later that day … she went on to share with me that she had lived in Mexico while her mother lived in California. This student had to go to school, work, and maintain a home for her eight younger siblings. Three years ago her mother brought her here to California, and here she is. She is a straight "A" student speaking English very well, soaking in information, and was well on her way to college and to being a success story.

> But … now, she is being taken out of my program. Worse than that, she is being taken out of school as a whole. Her mother is moving her to Las Vegas with no plans to enroll her in school. (Martinez, 2013, n.p.)

Fran is devastated.

Anzaldúa urged the generation of theories based on those whose knowledges are often excluded from and silenced by academic research. She further asserted that beyond creating theories, we need to find practical application for those theories. Anzaldúa advised that "we need to de-academize theory and to connect the community to the academy" (Anzaldúa, 1990, p. xxvi). Anzaldúa (2002) also noted that "Change requires more than words on a page—it takes perseverance, creative ingenuity and acts of love" (p. 574).

Through the persona of Fran Martinez, her own historical and cultural influences, and her dedication to working with youth from migrant families, we see illustrations of the de-academization of theory. Multiple examples of conocimiento theory appear as all the dimensions of the lives of migrant students and their tutor interconnect. Fran Martinez has documented memories from her childhood that influenced her strong feelings about her home language, her family, and her passions and interests. These experiences reflect the importance of viewing family, learning, and opportunities through conocimiento theory, and point to her passion for supporting Latino youth from all backgrounds, and especially from migrant families.

Anzaldúa might have smiled at Martinez's thoughts about an academic article she had been thinking about. Martinez said, "Reading articles makes us knowledgeable, and it is important to learn what others have found and concluded. But nothing beats personally working with these kids and firsthand verifying that what one is reading in academia is true" (Martinez, 2013, n.p.).

Martinez suggests that we can support migrant youth in spite of the struggles beyond their control by creating a positive environment and displaying respect for diversity and values. Her suggestions reveal work she has considered and internalized based on critical theory and critical literacy. The knowledge overlaps with exploring the knowledges of conocimiento theory. Critical theory stresses participation by all in the learning process, multiple sources of knowledge, and transformative action. Conocimiento theory stresses the merging of the individual and the collective, the academic and the social … the whole person. Martinez suggests having older students mentor the younger ones. This would give them a chance to be mentors, and share experiences and demonstrate trust. She notes that the teacher can personalize lessons based on the students' experiences. This can help the learners feel confident in the classroom. The teacher can implement assessments based on language proficiency that are appropriate to the students' academic needs. (This would be transformative for the teacher as well as the students.) It is also important that the teacher do research about the learners' culture and language. This can help open the communication between parents and the teacher.

Linking community resources (such as adult-education programs or existing parenting programs) and schools has the potential to create positive learning environments for both children and families (St. Clair, Jackson, & Zweiback, 2012). It is no secret that parent involvement is a huge factor in any child's education. Parents of migrant children suffer from the same challenges as their children: language and education barriers, and lack of confidence. Programs that help the parent are useful and necessary.

Despite all of the challenges that migrant students face due to their lifestyle, they also gain many advantages from the experiences their lifestyle entails. Having to adapt to new environments—a necessity for these students—is a skill that many people cannot grasp. These students also have the ability to solve problems on their own. They meet new challenges and are able to problem-solve and adapt with ease. Migrant students also have wide-ranging knowledge of cultural and geographical diversity. Using this knowledge and these skills, these students can develop confidence and a sense of self that can lead them toward a successful academic future. According to Anzaldúa, our muse for this work,

> To survive the Borderlands
> you must live sin fronteras
> be a crossroads. (1999, p. 195)

I argue that many of us do critique the failure of our current system of early care and education in the United States. However, at least here in the United States, our system is operating a rigid, very conservative (classist and racist) economic system that binds policy and programming. There is much to learn about protesting and influencing systemic change, but it is a long, slow process. And the children are only 2, 3, and 4 years old for a fleetingly short time. We have to figure out how to work with the children while, on parallel initiatives, changing the system.

Neuroscience and Early Childhood

In spite of the fact that there have been many venues and policy discussions in the past few years that connect recent neuroscience research with early childhood issues, the facts demand that we look beyond the superficial claims and go deeper into the research itself. As recently as the December 10, 2014, White House Summit on Early Childhood Education, noted invited panelists and speakers connected neuroscience research to rationales for supporting early education. Yet, as Penn (2014) acknowledges, "neuroscientific advances have been amazing. But it is still worth being cautious" (p. 14). She and others go deeper into the often casually drawn relationships between neuroscience research and issues in early childhood education. "There are no studies that related a particular kind of early childhood experience, other than gross abuse, to brain development—in fact, [there is] no discussion at all about what constitutes a good regime for young children" (Penn, 2014, p. 92). Kagan (1998) has been a persistent critic of the view that intervention in the first 3 years is singularly urgent. He argues that the evidence about brain research is used in a very cavalier way:

> Psychological determinists have assumed that every kiss, every lullaby, or scolding alters a child's brain in ways that will influence his future. But if slight changes in

synapses, like some amino acid substitutions, are without functional consequences, then every smile at an infant is not to be viewed as a bank deposit accumulating psychological dividends. (p. 20)

It is understandable that because of our passion, enthusiasm, and our commitment to the field, many of us want to "fill in the gaps" and make connections that we hope will play out in further research. However, we must ask questions about how depending on research that is not actually concluding what it is assumed to be concluding helps our cause of supporting early childhood. Another question that arises is, who is benefiting from these claims? Again, it seems that some of these claims are used in the complicated agendas of political and economic constituents to promote one program or another.

We see some possibilities in these pages, and at the same time, the complexities can seem overwhelming. On the one hand, we may overestimate the extent to which cultural patterns are shared and regular, yet, on the other hand, we underestimate the possibility of getting along without completely changing one way of life to match that of a different cultural group. Likewise, while pushing the possibilities of charting new paths for understanding, there is a desperate need for scholars, intellectuals, and human rights activists to challenge the current pervasive anti-intellectualism not only inside the broad field of education, but across American society and world societies. This is true especially in government realms, but it has permeated all institutions in the public spheres. Thus,

theoretical research becomes a political undertaking....Optimistic by profession, innocent by design, we teachers resist facing the fact that the historical present is an educational nightmare haunted by right-wing reactionaries and business-enamored politicians. (Pinar, 2004, p. 22)

In Chapter 1 of this book, the problem of equity for all children was raised in the discussion about the need for a participatory, responsive, and integrated curriculum and authentic assessment. The findings discussed and the case study excerpts of Juan, Melina, Julia, Kate, Leila, Fran, and others illustrate the importance of this on a day-to-day basis. For those of us working day-to-day with children, this is an important contribution. Yet, the issues are deeper, both in the United States and internationally. Many of us who work with families and children from all over the world, from a vast variety of circumstances, are concerned not only that childhood inequality is rampant around the world, but that this fact is accepted as a fact of life. Furthermore, the situation is perpetuated (unknowingly or intentionally) by many of the kinds of international aid programs serving young children and families.

The questions, then, don't stop with issues related to theoretical foundations in a multitude of contexts, how curriculum is created and delivered, and/or how assessment is carried out. These issues web together, back to questions of funding and provision of programs. Lloyd and Penn (2013), through their work at the University of East London and their edited book, document concern that availability, quality, and sustainability of publicly supported early childhood education and care may be at an important juncture in modern welfare states. They say that within childcare markets, because there is such inequality of parental incomes, equitable early childhood programming is in jeopardy. This is occurring despite worldwide acknowledgment of young children's rights, reflected in various UNESCO goals (2006). Lloyd and Penn (2013) continue the thread of discussion and critical thinking about funding, markets, and the rationale for it all in Chapter 6.

References

Anzaldúa, G. (1990). *Haciendo caras/Making face, making soul: Creative and critical perspectives by women of color.* San Francisco: Aunt Lute Press.

Anzaldúa, G. (1999). *Borderlands/La frontera: The new mestiza* (2nd ed.). San Francisco: Aunt Lute Press.

Anzaldúa, G. (2002). Now let us shift…the path of conocimiento…inner work, public acts. In G. Anzaldúa & A. Keating (Eds.), *This bridge we call home: Radical visions for transformation* (pp. 540–578). New York: Routledge.

Dahlberg, G., Moss, P. M., & Pence, A. (2013). *Beyond quality in early childhood education and care: Languages of evaluation.* New York: Routledge.

Hérnandez-Ávila, I. (2000). Gloria Anzaldúa. In Keating, AnaLouise (Ed.), *Interviews/Intrevista* (p. 177). New York and London: Routledge.

Kagan, J. (1998). *Three seductive ideas.* Cambridge, MA: Harvard University Press.

Lloyd, E., & Penn, H. (Eds.). (2013). *Childcare markets: Can they deliver an equitable service?* Bristol, UK: Policy Press.

Martinez, F. (2013). FM personal research journal. Unpublished manuscript.

Nelson, K. (2009) *Young minds in social worlds: Experience, meaning and memory.* Cambridge, MA: Harvard University Press.

Penn, H. (2014). *Understanding early childhood: Issues and controversies* (3rd ed.). Berkshire, UK: Open University Press.

Pinar, W. (2004). *What is curriculum theory?* Mahwah, NJ: Lawrence Erlbaum Associates.

Quintero, E. P. (2012). Early childhood collaborations: Learning from migrant families and children. In R. W. Blake & B. E. Blake (Eds.), *Becoming a teacher: Using narrative as reflective practice, a cross-disciplinary approach* (pp. 168–189). New York: Peter Lang.

Quintero, E. P. (2013). Research journal. Unpublished manuscript.

Quintero, E. P. (2014). Juan, Melina, and friends: Guides for reconceptualizing readiness. In W. Parnell & J. M. Iorio (Eds.), *Reconceptualizing readiness in early childhood education* (pp. 179–190). New York: Springer.

St. Clair, L., Jackson, B., & Zweiback, R. (2012). Six years later: Effect of family involvement training on the language skills of children from migrant families. *School Community Journal, 22*(1), 9–20.

UNESCO. (2006). *UNESCO programme for the elimination of poverty, especially extreme poverty.* Retrieved from http://unesdoc.unesco.org/images/0015/001506/150618eo.pdf

Yoshikawa, H., Weiland, C., Brooks-Gunn, J., Burchinal, M. R., Espinosa, L. M., Gormley, W. T., ... Zaslow, M. J. (2013). *Investing in our future: The evidence base on preschool education.* Ann Arbor, MI: Society for Research in Child Development. Retrieved from http://www.srcd.org/policy-media/policy-updates/meetings-briefings/investing-our-future-evidence-base-preschool.

6

WHAT ARE CHILDCARE MARKETS AND HOW ARE MEASURES OF QUALITY RELATED TO FUNDING?

[M]ore than 80% of childcare provision in the UK is now provided by for-profit entrepreneurs. (Lloyd & Penn, 2013, p. 20)

This is true not only in the United Kingdom, but also across much of the English-speaking world in countries with a variety of economic policies. If that were not disturbing enough, for the implications some of us could draw, there is almost no debate in these countries about whether or not this is equitable, efficient, and humane. Early care and education services are often very closely linked to other social and educational services and economic policy. Governments often seem to find it necessary to create a balance between serving the interests of parents and children and the interests of the state itself. Childcare markets form a part of a mixed economy, as other human services do. In other words, fully state-funded early childhood care and education programs are often available and operate in parallel with privately provided services in some markets (Lloyd & Penn, 2013).

Lloyd and Penn (2013), through their work at the Cass School of Education and Communities, University of East London, and their research at the International Centre for the Study of the Mixed Economy of Childcare, document their concerns. Availability, quality, and sustainability of publicly supported early care and education are extremely complicated in modern states and nations. They say that within childcare markets, because there is such inequality of parental income, equitable early care and education is in jeopardy. This is occurring despite worldwide acknowledgment of young children's rights, reflected by various international aid organizations and UNESCO goals (2006).

Lloyd (2013) says, "One particular option for addressing these policy conundrums is the promotion of a market-based approach to the provision of early childhood education and care" (p. 3) To repeat, childcare markets form a part of a mixed economy, as other human services do. In other words, fully state-funded early childhood care and education programs are often available and operate in parallel with privately provided services in some markets.

How did we get here? Why are societies in the complicated situation of scrambling to provide what on many levels is a human right? Penn (2013) explains that around the world, in terms of supporting early childhood services, "Governments have chosen either a supply-side model of expansion, in which money has been given directly to services, or a demand-led model of expansion, in which money is given to parents to buy childcare" (p. 23). The supply-side model is often adapted to accommodate the needs of working parents, and in some countries nonprofit agencies are awarded grant funding to offer services. The demand-led model provides to low-income parents direct funds as subsidies to purchase early care and education services at market prices.

A mixed economy is an economy that includes a variety of private and government controls; reflecting characteristics of both capitalism and socialism, there are elements of both public and private enterprise. The bottom-line questions are: Who provides early care and education? Who funds early care and education? Who uses early care and education, and what are the intended and unintended consequences?

A Mixed-Economy Model for Childcare

There is no evidence that the mixed economy model works—in fact, it doesn't work for low-income families (Lloyd & Penn, 2013). In childcare markets, parents are proxy consumers on behalf of their children, who are the actual consumers of the service. Parental choice may be supported with the help of public subsidies such as tax credits or vouchers, as long as their income remains below any caps set by governments (Warner & Gradus, 2011). Childcare markets are now the dominant models for early childhood programs in European countries and in many English-speaking nations, including the United States, Canada, and Australia, and countries on the African continent and in the Asia Pacific region.

"Neoliberal countries have almost all adopted a demand-led model, since it is based on the primacy of personal choice" (Penn, 2013, p. 23). Again, neoliberalism is an approach to economics and social services in which the control and responsibility for economic factors shifts from the public to the private sector ("Neoliberalism," n.d.). In many societies with neoliberal approaches, this thinking about "markets" is oddly equated with democracy. The thinking is that any individual can compete in the marketplace and earn money without much regulation. Consequently, a neoliberal approach is one in which equality and fairness are not prevalent goals. Instead, there is rhetoric of equality of opportunity, which may mean no more than a freedom to compete in an unequal society. Economic rationales offer a variety of positions on childcare, depending on the stance adopted. Joseph Stiglitz (2009), a renowned U.S. economist, explains that neoliberal economic theories present a perspective about the economic organization of society with the emphasis on competition and productivity.

In the United States, Schmit and Matthews, from the Center for Law and Social Policy, and Smith and Robins, from the National Center for Children in Poverty, document the stark realities of inequity in poor children's access to early care and education (Schmit, Matthews, Smith, & Robbins, 2013). Their research, through multiple measures, highlights the complex mix of weak policies and provisions for children who could benefit the most from early care and education (Dearing, McCartney, & Taylor, 2009), but in fact are not being served.

An alternative can be seen in France, where a state-funded and state-provided early care and education system has existed for over 60 years. The government considers that there are strong economic grounds for considering early care and education services as contributing to the "public good," which justifies public investment in the services and in their infrastructure (Lloyd, 2013). Investment in early care and education services and the infrastructure is considered a key for assuring universal access to equal services for all children regardless of their parents' socioeconomic status, ethnic background, geographical location, or health status (Cleveland & Krashinski, 2004; Leseman, 2009; Lloyd & Penn, 2013).

In the United States, the economist James Heckman is frequently quoted on the topic of funding for early care and education. He argues that investing in early childhood is a good thing, and he seems to be a supporter of early childhood services. However, in spite of the early childhood field receiving welcome attention and publicity from professionals from outside the discipline, a closer look at Heckman's arguments reveals that his advocacy is limited to particular circumstances, rather than reflecting any kind of all-encompassing benevolence in favor of early childhood services. Penn (2014) explicitly points out that the returns-on-investment argument that Heckman makes focuses on the economic productivity of individuals and the situations in which it might be maximized. Much of the rationale for Heckman is that early childhood funding will ensure social mobility for children throughout their lives. Social mobility in which community? What assumptions and values are attached to this "mobility"? We understand that human capital theory, upon which Heckman and many other Western economists base their advocacy ideas for funding of early childhood programs, values individual economic productivity as the skill base that ensures economic growth. However, critics of human capital theory bring up the difficulty in measuring both the individual economic productivity of workers and also the actual amount of economic growth that results (Marshall, 1998).

Stiglitz (2006) questions cost-benefit analysis studies and maintains that poverty on a huge scale is structural, not a matter of personal failings, and can be addressed only by rethinking ideas of economic justice and redistribution on a global scale. Going back to the case study of Juan and his family, who are in the precarious situation of sharing a one-room apartment with several families, including adults and children, we must ask questions about economics and policy and the stark influence of these on the lives of young children. The Children's Defense Fund (2015) documents that there are 14.7 million poor children in the United States. The United States ranks thirty-fourth in relative child poverty in the world—ahead only of Romania, whose economy is 99% smaller than ours.

In our qualitative study, as reported in Chapter 1, early childhood studies teacher education student participants are teachers, student teachers, and their pupils, pre-kindergarten to age 8, including children who are dual-language learners and children with special needs. All teacher participants are actively involved in working with children in either a student teaching or teaching situation. Some programs are in urban schools, some are in rural schools, and most programs (82%) served families in poverty.

In almost every program (96%), children who are dual-language learners participate. How do our participants fit into these international discussions about funding of early care and education? I can report that recurring discussions in our university classes in Southern California repeatedly focus on the very young children who are locked in cars beside the strawberry fields where their parents are picking fruit. What is human capital worth when this is childhood?

Equity and Quality Connections to Funding Situations

Again, the question that must be raised is whether or not a childcare market is a reliable and equitable way of delivering early care and education. For neoliberal countries, the risks and complications involved in allowing entrepreneurs to provide early care and education are either ignored or seen as acceptable, or an illogical combination of the two. Lloyd and Penn (2013) maintain that "Viewing childcare as a commodity to be bought and sold undermines equity and quality, and regulation has to be comprehensive and wide-reaching in order to try and compensate for these failings" (p. 34). This leads us to the next very complicated set of issues about quality in early childhood programming.

Usually, requirements for health and safety, space, staff education, staff-child ratios, and curricula vary considerably among countries. This is especially true where businesses compete in a fragmented system with little or no monitoring. Peter Moss (2013) asks us to consider

> what happens when democracy becomes sclerotic and a society falls prey to fundamentalist dogma that claims to have the right answer for everything: in short, when neoliberal capitalism becomes a hegemonic system of thought and practice, with its unswerving belief in the virtues of markets and the private, of competition and inequality, and of calculation and individual choice. (p. 191)

Moss (2013) illuminates the contradictions of the mixed childcare market in the United Kingdom. He explains that policy in the UK developed prescriptive regulations, combining standards and curriculum for the entire age range of the early years—The Early Years Foundation Stage. It is a legal framework of practice guidelines, consisting of two volumes of early learning goals, educational programs for each of six areas of "learning and development," and assessment arrangements, culminating in the Early Years Foundation Stage Profile (Moss, 2013). Furthermore, the implementation of the curriculum was to be certified by a state agency. In addition, there is a professional development system for childcare workers based on a detailed set of "national occupational standards" and criteria for how the workers are to be assessed (Moss, 2013). Is this hegemonic? Does the system itself become dogma in this case?

Moss goes on to elaborate:

> Opening up resistance to the dictatorship of no alternative, and therefore, opening up to alternative means going back to asking and seeking answers to what have been termed "critical" or "political" questions. Chantal Mouffe, to take one example, argues that "contrary to what neoliberal ideologists would like us to believe, political questions are not mere technical issues to be solved by experts...." [T]he mere act of asking political questions helps pull politics free of its collapse into economics and re-asserts education as first, and foremost, a political (and also ethical) practice. (Moss, 2013, p. 201)

Moss believes our questions about providing early care and education should include: What is the purpose of early care and education? What are the fundamental values of early care and education? What are the ethics of early care and education? What do we mean by "learning" and "knowledge"? What is our image of the child, the educator, the early childhood center? What do we want for our children? (Moss, 2013).

In Chapter 1 of this book, the problem of equity for all children was raised in the discussion about the need for a participatory, responsive, and integrated curriculum and authentic assessment. The findings discussed and the case study excerpts of Juan, Melina, Julia, Kate, and others illustrate the importance of this on a day-to-day basis. Penn (2014) makes the connection among politics, policy, practice, and research. If we analyze the current mantra for evidence-based practice and policy, we see problems. There is a conflict when a government wishes to introduce a policy and wants the research to back it up, and the researchers have evidence that is not supportive of the policy the government wants. In the United States we saw this fiasco during the years of No Child Left Behind, when faulty research was promoted to back up the policy.

Intersection of Policy, Practice, and Culture: An International Example

To illustrate the intersection of issues related to providing early care and education policies, governmental realities, and cultural values and assumptions that directly affect practice, it is illustrative to briefly look at the past few decades of early care and education policy and practice in New Zealand. During the 1970s and 1980s in New Zealand, "Various coalitions of unionists, feminists, childcare activists, and Maoris all argued for a more fundamental rethink of early education and care services, although through differing perspectives" (Penn, 2011, p. 20). In 1998 the Labour prime minister, David Lange, issued a plan, *Before Five*, to try to reconcile care and education in an education framework. This document, following the bilingual, bicultural curriculum *Te Whāriki*, gave unprecedented attention to the needs of the Maori community in the *Te Kōhanga Reo* (Maori-run centers). Working groups were set up to consider the implications for training, curricula, regulation, and funding, and quality was tied to a charter for community/parent participation.

Then, politics happened. Lange resigned and a conservative government returned and curtailed many developments.

> The curriculum developments, perhaps the most radical innovations remaining, were worked on by Maori as well as white academics and activists, and codified into a national curriculum *Te Whāriki* (a woven mat). This took as its central principles well-being, belonging, contribution, communication and exploration—a move away from the traditional English curricula of physical, intellectual, emotional, and social skills. Margaret Carr, who had been involved in the creation of *Te Whāriki*, also developed an approach to assessment called *Learning Stories*, also widely cited as an alternative to more conventional assessment tests or views of quality. (Penn, 2011, p. 21)

Unfortunately, in spite of these initiatives and intentions, New Zealand has not changed as much as many of us watching had hoped (May & Mitchell, 2009). The bilingual, bicultural curriculum has been centralized and professional development is ongoing for early childhood workers. Yet, in New Zealand, as in so many countries in this decade, there is a move to demand-led funding.

This example from New Zealand also shows an important reality that we are struggling with internationally. Policy makers and often politicians declare and define characteristics of "quality" without having much experience with early care and education and with no idea of the changing influences of demographics on families' childrearing practices, family priorities, and what Nelson (2009) calls the "mind-culture symbiosis." Her research advocates for a developmental-systems approach where "meaning belongs first to persons, and personal meaning filters cultural offerings. Thus the symbiosis grows in developmental time, at least partially through the openness accorded to culture by the child's own mind" (p. 267).

What Is "Quality" and Who Decides?

Going back to our discussion in Chapter 1, historically in the United States definitions of quality in early care and education have included multiple measures that describe indicators of curriculum and classroom interactions, and requirements of specific programs and state policy aspects with the intention of promoting children's development in various domains (Dunn, 1993). However, because of the multitude of perspectives on which indicators are most important, the resulting definitions of quality are often broad or nonspecific (Layzer & Goodson, 2006). Furthermore, to repeat Dahlberg, Moss, and Pence's (2013) warning,

> Theories used to describe children's development have a tendency to start functioning as if they were "true" models of reality, becoming a kind of abstract map spread over the actual territory of children's development and upbringing. Instead of being seen as socially constructed representations of a complex reality, one selected way of how to describe the world, these theories seem to become the territory itself. (pp. 38–39)

Consequently, in response to such underlying disagreements about even the broad definitions, some researchers have conceptualized early care and education quality in terms of global quality with two primary components—"structural" and "process" quality. Examples of indicators of structural quality include classroom materials, curriculum, teacher education, and teacher-child ratio. These indicators are often the regulated aspects of classrooms and programs. Indicators of process quality focus on the more dynamic aspects of early childhood education. These dynamic aspects include human interactions, activities, materials, learning opportunities, and health and safety routines. In every classroom where there are children telling stories of cows and horses in their home language, as Melina was, or where friends are negotiating, in their home language, who will get to play with the slippers, will these rich interactions be considered examples of "quality"? Process quality is typically measured by observing the experiences in the centers and classrooms and rating the multiple dimensions of the program, such as teacher-child interactions, type of instruction, room environment, materials, relationships with parents, and health and safety routines. Do the multiple dimensions include space to acknowledge discussions and thinking about cows, horses, and slippers? These are not flippant questions; they are fundamental and contentious questions that must be considered.

In October 2013 Yoshikawa, et al. reported that "only a minority of preschool programs are observed to provide excellent quality and levels of instructional support" (p. 1). What is "quality," and what is "instructional support"? Juan needed exceptional instructional support, and the complex qualitative nature of the assessment done by Mia and the other teachers was absolutely necessary. In reality, the instructional support he received was at such a deep intellectual and risk-taking level (on the part of the staff) that it boggles the mind that this wouldn't be on a nationwide checklist of desired examples.

The Politics of Quality

There has been talk and some action by the Obama administration, which identified as high priorities both strengthening the quality of early learning and development programs and increasing access to them, especially for children with high needs. Basically, the voiced intention is to get more children with high needs in higher-quality programs, and to develop integrated systems, including a framework to support quality improvement. Across the country for the past 15 years there have been many quality-rating improvement systems (QRIS) developed. The QRIS in California shows the three core areas of child development, teachers and teaching, and program and environment. But where did the QRIS come from? The California Department of Education drew on nationally recognized standards that lead to improved learning and development outcomes for children, including:

1. Relevant recommendations from the legislatively created California Early Learning Quality Improvement System (CAEL QIS) Advisory Committee's final report.

2. Quality Criteria components from the First 5 California Power of Preschool Program and the Educare model, and evidence-based Early Learning and Development Program for at-risk children.
3. Standards and practices from Head Start.
4. A rich body of scientific knowledge on quality elements, and effectiveness factors," associated with improving child outcomes and found to consistently produce positive impacts. (California Early Learning Quality Improvement System Advisory Committee, 2014)

We have discussed critical questions throughout these chapters of each of these four categories. I would advocate that we address each area (and more) and ask what we know now based on new contexts of children and families, new information from international early education programs, and most importantly, from sustained, consistent, longitudinal *listening to* children like Juan, Melina, and Fernando and their families.

Many counties in the state of California have been working on a related version of QRIS for their home counties. Our county, Ventura County, has been working on a system for almost ten years. A collaborative group comprised of professionals from early care and education programs around the county, parents, and staff from the Ventura Office of Education's Early Childhood Division has met four to six times a year to debate the issues and the most equitable way to implement the QRIS. The elements that are rated are child development and school readiness, developmental and health screenings, early childhood educator qualifications, effective teacher child interactions (CLASS), environmental rating scales, ratios and group sizes, and director qualifications. If a program is successful in reaching an acceptable rating, there are improvement tools and resources, and the result is improved quality programs for children and informed parents and children ready to succeed in kindergarten (Ventura County Office of Education, 2014).

These 15 years of quality initiatives became the foundation for what is now known as the Quality Rating Improvement System (QRIS) in California and in many states around the United States. QRIS has created an umbrella for other quality initiative (QI) efforts, including initiatives to address the "school readiness gap." However, very few people are asking who is responsible for this "readiness gap"—the schools, or the children and their families? And fewer people are asking just what our assumptions are about what "school readiness" is or isn't. Many families believe that school readiness has many

more dynamics than knowing the alphabet, knowing number symbol corre-
spondence, and writing one's name.

Imagine the discussions that have passed and are yet to come given the
critical questions addressed in this study. Has the work been helpful in many
cases? Of course. Do we in the field still feel uncomfortable, or downright
disagree with aspects of the premises, assumptions, and implementation?
Of course.

Measurements of Quality

And again, all these discussions about quality often avoid the issue of how
quality is measured. In Chapter 4 of this book we mentioned just a few measurement tools used in California and the United States and in some international programs. One of the most widely used, heavily marketed tools
mentioned, which is used widely in the international arena, is the environmental rating scale. There is research (Sheridan, Giota, Han, & Kwon,
2009) that documents that the environmental rating scales do not adequately
address what is known about either (a) cultural differences in perceptions of
quality or (b) validity of rating scales. The findings of this study that investi-
gates the environmental rating scales used in South Korea and Sweden shows
that there are differences in preschool quality that could be interpreted as
culturally based. The results highlight structural aspects of preschool quality,
such as resources of space, as being important for overall quality.

Quality, Curriculum, and Teacher Education

Governments institutionalize, by intention and by default, early childhood
services. Of course, curriculum frameworks differ among countries, and are
usually chosen because they correspond with key goals of service in the particular countries. In some countries, the process of choosing frameworks
involves a participatory consultation process with different stakeholders. In
the United States, the processes (and results) differ between federally and
state-sponsored services and private services. And among and within the
50 states, there is great variation in the process of choosing and the results.
Curricula highlight also the different policy, political, and economic situations in different countries. In Flanders, Belgium, all nursery education
from 2½ years of age on is provided in nursery classes attached to schools

(Penn, 2011). In Italy, Reggio Emilia is the ongoing result of over 25 years of investment by a small socialist municipality that has maintained the freedom to experiment and develop its early care and education model. The result has been a pedagogical theory and model that is known and borrowed to varying degrees worldwide (Rinaldi, 2005). The Swedish curriculum has direct commitment to equality throughout society reflected in their curriculum. As mentioned previously, *Te Whāriki* is the bicultural, bilingual curriculum created through a collaboration of Maori and non-Maori early care and education specialists. In the United States there are multiple examples of curricula for early care and education. In the private market, which still believes that the universal needs of children are the same during their early years, curriculum has become a product in the competitive publishing market. Some companies (such as the producers and marketers of the *High Scope* curriculum) are not-for-profit companies that maintain that their curriculum is ideal for all marginalized and impoverished communities. There are other curricula sponsored by various groups such as the National Association for the Education of Young Children. They sponsor an emergent curriculum, which is interesting in comparison with some marketed by for-profit companies in a standardized format, and at least founded on the premise that young children learn through play and build their own curricula. The premise is similar to that of the Reggio Emilia curriculum, with an important difference: Reggio teachers in Italy, courtesy of their program, have opportunities for critical and consistent professional development as a part of their teaching routine. Teachers in the United States, for the most part, don't have that support. It is not uncommon in the United States for very wealthy private corporations to offer employer-sponsored early care and education for employees' children and use the emergent curriculum model. And it is not uncommon for teachers and assistant teachers here to make minimum wage, have no opportunity for advancement in the company, and virtually no opportunities for professional development.

Elizabeth Jones (2012), the developer of the emergent curriculum, maintains that the curriculum is based upon the play of children. She says that teachers and children co-construct the curriculum based on children's interests and materials in the environment. This is a very similar premise, on the surface, to the one that I advocate in Chapters 2 and 3 in this book. There is an important difference: While Jones (2012) always intended for teachers to have ongoing support for interpreting the children's interests and needs in the dynamic process of making the curriculum, this most often does not happen.

The curriculum is used in both publicly and privately funded programs and mixed markets, but across the board, the budgets of the programs don't support sufficient, if any, professional development. There is another big difference between emergent curriculum and the integrated curriculum I propose which uses a critical theory framework. Emergent curriculum is based upon the constructivist theory of Piaget, Vygotsky, and others. As discussed in both Chapter 2 and Chapter 5 in this book, teacher education students participating in the current study are pushed to ask critical questions about theoretical information, theories of child development, contexts, and learning in order to frame creation of a more appropriate curriculum for each group of children.

The Politics of Leadership

Leadership issues are beginning to arise in the field of early care and education as more and more educators are furthering their educations. For example, as mentioned in Chapters 1 to 4 in this book, many of us, both inside and outside the United States. have critical questions about the leadership of the National Association for the Education of Young Children. Penn's (2011) analysis of the NAEYC's list of child development "truths" and their rigid relationship to practice is that the "leadership" of this huge professional organization is saying there is a magic formula to teaching and learning.

Penn (2011) reports that the Organisation for Economic Co-operation and Development, whose aim is to promote policies to improve economic and social well-being of people around the world, cautions targeting vulnerable children. In reviewing issues of access, childcare quality, and poverty in more than 20 countries, their report *Starting Strong II (2006)* succinctly concludes that service for the poor is a poor service.

Service for the "poor"…the whole idea is very complicated. Recently, at an advisory board meeting for an agency that administers nationwide grant-funded programs for "poor children and families," there was a conversation in which board members were asked why they chose to volunteer their time and energy in the organization: "I want to support our agency because we do things for these parents and children that they can't do themselves." Oh my. And this is from a well-educated community leader. Certainly, the emotion comes from a place of empathy and care, but really? Does this not seem patronizing? Does this comment not scream for an analysis of the structural causes of poverty mentioned by Stiglitz earlier in this chapter?

Finally, it is important to note that in December 2014, President Obama convened a White House Summit on Early Childhood Education in the United States. Advocates and experts were brought together for the White House Summit on Early Education with the intention of highlighting leadership in support of early education in the United States. Leaders shared what they consider and call "best practices" in building the public-private partnerships to promote and expand early education in communities across the country. While it is true that private and philanthropic organizations committed to new programs were present at the White House summit, if the intention was to provide more high-quality preschool and early learning programs, then the intention came up lacking. This is in spite of the $330 million in new actions from corporate and philanthropic leaders to expand programs and enhance the quality of early education for thousands of children. Many believe the approaches being promoted don't address the stark inequities in the United States.

It is good that $750 million in new federal grant awards were announced by Secretaries Duncan and Burwell to support early learning for more than 63,000 additional children across the country (White House Press Office, 2014). But where does this money come from? And while these investments purport to expand high-quality preschool and increase the programming for infant and toddlers, what are the guarantees of "quality"? Is the definition of "quality" in line with parents' hopes and dreams for their children? And the newly launched "Invest in Us" is a classic mixed-market Band-Aid of a new initiative of partnerships with private philanthropic leaders, in response to the president's call for action. It seems to be another, perhaps well-intentioned collaboration in which the poor and the privileged have access to separate and unequal programming.

References

California Early Learning Quality Improvement System Advisory Committee. (2014). *Dream big for our youngest children. Executive summary*. Retrieved from http://www.cde.ca.gov/sp/cd/re/documents/fnlrptexecsummary.pdf

Children's Defense Fund. (2015). *Ending child poverty now*. Washington, DC: Author. Retrieved from http://www.childrensdefense.org/library/PovertyReport/EndingChildPovertyNow.html#sthash.9p5ySGOC.dpuf

Cleveland, G., & Krashinski, M. (2004). *Financing ECEC services in OECD countries*. Paris: Organisation for Economic Cooperation and Development.

Dahlberg, G., Moss, P. M., & Pence, A. (2013). *Beyond quality in early childhood education and care: Languages of evaluation*. New York: Routledge.

Dearing, E., McCartney, K., & Taylor, B. A. (2009). Does higher quality early child care promote low-income children's math and reading achievement in middle childhood? *Child Development, 80*(5),1329–1349.

Dunn, J. (1993). *Young children's close relationships*. London: Sage.

Jones, E. (2012). Our proud heritage: The emergence of emergent curriculum, *Young Children, 67*(2), 66–68.

Layzer, J. I., & Goodson, B. D. (2006). The "quality" of early care and education settings. *Evaluation Review, 30*(5), 556–576.

Leseman, P. (2009). *Taking social and cultural inequalities through early childhood education and care in Europe*. Brussels: European Commission.

Lloyd, E. (2013). Childcare markets: An introduction. In E. Lloyd & H. Penn (Eds.), *Childcare markets: Can they deliver an equitable service?* (pp. 3–18). Bristol, UK: Policy Press.

Lloyd, E., & Penn, H. (Eds.). (2013). *Childcare markets: Can they deliver an equitable service?* Bristol, UK: Policy Press.

Marshall, G. (1998). Human-capital theory. In G. Marshall (Ed.), *A dictionary of sociology* (2nd ed.). New York: Oxford University Press. Retrieved from http://www.encyclopedia.com/doc/1O88-Humancapitaltheory.html

May, H., & Mitchell, L. (2009). *Politics in the playground. The world of early childhood education in New Zealand*. Dunedin, NZ: Otago University Press.

Moss, P. (2013). Need markets be the only show in town? In E. Lloyd & H. Penn (Eds.), *Childcare markets: Can they deliver an equitable service?* (pp. 191–208). Bristol, UK: Policy Press.

"Neoliberalism." (n.d.). *Investopedia*. Retrieved from http://www.investopedia.com/terms/n/neoliberalism.asp

Organisation for Economic Cooperation and Development. (2006). *Starting strong II: Early childhood education and care*. Paris: Author.

Penn, H. (2011). *Quality in early childhood services: An international perspective*. Berkshire, UK: Open University Press.

Penn, H. (2013). Childcare markets: Do they work? In E. Lloyd & H. Penn (Eds.), *Childcare markets: Can they deliver an equitable service?* (pp. 19–42). Bristol, UK: Policy Press.

Penn, H. (2014). *Understanding early childhood: Issues and controversies* (3rd ed.). Berkshire, UK: Open University Press.

Rinaldi, C. (2005). *In dialogue with Reggio Emilia: Listening, researching, and learning*. New York: Routledge.

Schmit, S., Matthews, H., Smith, S., & Robbins, T. (2013). *Investing in young children: A fact sheet on early care and education participation, access, and quality*. New York: National Center for Children in Poverty; Washington, DC: Center for Law and Social Policy.

Sheridan, S., Giota, J., Han, Y., & Kwon, J. (2009). A cross-cultural study of preschool quality in South Korea and Sweden: ECERS evaluations. *Early Childhood Research Quarterly, 24*(2), 142–156.

Stiglitz, J. (2006). *Making globalization work*. London: Penguin.

Stiglitz, J. (2009). *Report on the commission on measurement of economic performance and social justice*. Paris: French Presidency.

UNESCO Goals (2006). *UNESCO programme for the elimination of poverty, especially extreme poverty*. Retrieved from http://unesdoc.unesco.org/images/0015/001506/150618eo.pdf

Ventura County Office of Education. (2014). *Ventura County quality rating and improvement system QRIS*. Retrieved from http://www.vcoe.org/Portals/VcssoPortals/ecp/05.2014_QRISwoNotes.pdf

Warner, Mildred E., & Gradus, Raymond H. J. M. (2011). The consequences of implementing a child care voucher scheme: Evidence from Australia, the Netherlands and the USA. *Social Policy and Administration, 45*(5), pp. 569–592.

White House Press Office. (2014). *Invest in the US: The White House Summit on Early Childhood Education*. Retrieved from http://www.whitehouse.gov/the-press-office/2014/12/10/fact-sheet-invest-us-white-house-summit-early-childhood-education

Yoshikawa, H., Weiland, C., Brooks-Gunn, J., Burchinal, M. R., Espinosa, L. M., Gormley, W. T., ...Zaslow, M. J. (2013). *Investing in our future: The evidence base on preschool education*. Ann Arbor, MI: Society for Research in Child Development. Retrieved from http://www.srcd.org/policy-media/policy-updates/meetings-briefings/investing-our-future-evidence-base-preschool

7

THROUGH THE LENS OF
MIGRANT FAMILIES

Clearly, all the issues discussed in this book relate to all children. Because of specific aspects of the issues and the urgent conditions under which many migrant families live, it is important to show how these issues affect migrant families and their young children. Throughout the discussions of the overlapping and intersecting issues, the findings show that context is of supreme importance in terms of children's experience, safety, relationships, and learning. Thus, context—demographic, social emotional, cultural, cognitive, and needs-based perceptions—underlies all curriculum initiatives, assessment practices, policy, and access. These realities are highlighted by the complexities of many children in the United States and across the world whose families have had to emigrate from their historical homelands.

Sadly, no international migration institution or mechanism manages the rights of people who move between countries. At the national level, policies tend to focus overwhelmingly on the legal exclusion of unauthorized migrants. As population and poverty trends continue to further divide the world into stark categories of overpopulated, young, and poor states on one hand, and wealthy, aging, and declining population states on the other, migratory pressures will only intensify, making the need for a policy framework to guide this phenomenon ever more urgent. These needs for policy considerations directly affect education.

To begin, I would like to bring back a critical comment by Helen Penn (2011) about an often-heard rationale for the funding of and access to early care and education. The rationale is articulated as "Early education benefits all young children, enhances dispositions for learning, and socializes them for starting school, especially children from poor and migrant families" (p. 46). Penn clarifies her position:

> The stimulation of the brain through "appropriate" caregiving (that is, by the carer talking, singing, and reading to very young children) is said to develop neural networks and promote brain growth....There is no direct neuroscientific evidence to back up the claim that teaching mothers and carers how to stimulate their children makes a significant difference to long-term outcomes....Most neuroscientists point to the extreme complexity of the brain and caution against such extrapolation. (Penn, 2011, p. 46)

Of course, Penn's position does not mean that she doesn't support parents and caregivers learning to, and continuing to, talk, sing, and read to their young children. She is cautioning us all about believing that the current available neuroscience research shows that this is enough, that that is all children need to be just fine. These practices are good for children, *and* children still need food, shelter, and parents who have time to be with them as opposed to working three jobs to buy food. And we need state, national, and international policies to protect and accommodate families when their only option is to migrate to a new place.

Children Fleeing Central America Arriving in the United States

In the United States in summer 2014, roughly 1,000 new students from Central America—mostly from Honduras, Guatemala, and El Salvador, where gangs sometimes control entire neighborhoods and towns—were enrolled in Los Angeles Unified School District when school started in August. Debra Duardo, director of health and human services at the L.A. district office, says, "It's tough to get an exact count of the new Central American students who arrived alone or are with family and are in the process of gaining legal status" (Fujita, 2014, p. 1).

One family at Duardo's school is Kenia Bran and her two children, who fled Honduras after gang members killed Bran's husband: "They killed my husband, then threatened us," she says. "We had to leave." Now, after being smuggled north and getting detained at the U.S. border temporarily, the family is in Los Angeles with Bran's mother, who moved to the United States years ago. Even as they try to find a way to stay in the United States legally, one thing is clear: The kids need to be in school.

Duardo has worked for the district for years, but has never encountered such a wave of newly arrived students with such violent pasts. "In all the crises I've dealt with in this district—and as a social worker myself—I've never experienced such extreme disregard for human life and such violence," she says (Fujita, 2014, p. 2). Duardo says the sheer number of new students is one challenge, but schools also have to deal with the language issues and emotional trauma that come with the new arrivals (Fujita, 2014). Counselor Leticia López says problems often arise months after the start of the school year, after the initial excitement of living in a new country wears off. Some students suffer from recurring nightmares about their experiences at detention centers; others break into crying spells throughout the day (Fujita, 2014).

The child migration surge (to the United States) began in 2012 but spiked to unprecedented proportions during one year from 2014 to 2015. Government agencies have grappled with costs and challenges while attracting intense national media and political attention for most of the summer of 2014. In the absence of new funding from Congress, the Obama administration diverted funds from other Department of Homeland Security (DHS) operations to meet immediate costs. It also announced policy changes to address the situation at the border, including accelerated immigration hearings for the child and family arrivals, transfer of immigration judges to border areas, a program to provide legal counsel to some unaccompanied minors, and public service campaigns aimed at discouraging future flows.

On March 1, 2003, the Homeland Security Act of 2002 Section 462 transferred responsibilities for the care and placement of unaccompanied alien children (UAC) from the commissioner of the Immigration and Naturalization Service to the director of the Office of Refugee Resettlement (ORR). Since then, ORR has cared for more than 92,000 UAC, incorporating child welfare values as well as the principles and provisions established by the Flores Agreement in 1997 and the Trafficking Victims Protection Act of 2000 and its reauthorization acts, the William Wilberforce Trafficking Victims Protection

Reauthorization Acts (TVPRA) of 2005 and 2008 (Chishti, Hipsman, & Bui, 2014). Unaccompanied children apprehended by DHS immigration officials, are transferred to the care and custody of ORR, who are tasked with placement decisions, considering the best interests of the UAC to ensure placement in the least restrictive setting possible while in federal custody. ORR takes into consideration the unique nature of each UAC's situation and incorporates child welfare principles when making placement, clinical, case management, and release decisions (Chishti, Hipsman, & Bui, 2014).

Public Radio International's *The World* reported that, in part because of the numbers of unaccompanied minors at the United States border, many of the children are being sent home. The journey from Central America to the United States, crossing the border illegally, is dangerous. And so is going back home. This is a disturbing new element in the U.S. immigration crisis that's left thousands of women and children caught at the border awaiting deportation. Campbell (2014) quotes Jude Joffe-Block, a reporter for KJZZ in Phoenix who travelled to El Salvador to find out what awaits migrants who are forced to return home. She reports that numbers of people could return to their home countries in the coming weeks and months, but "These countries aren't set up for that right now" (Campbell, 2014, p. 1).

The United States knows that this is true, and is making American aid money available to Honduras, Guatemala, and El Salvador to improve their infrastructures so that they will be prepared when more women and children are sent back to their countries of origin on planes (Campbell, 2014). However, in many cases, what children are returning to are the same terrible conditions that caused them to flee in the first place.

A Global Reality

A teacher education student who had done an independent study during a study abroad experience investigated the situation of unaccompanied minors who arrived as asylum seekers. She was interested in the work done by the Refugee Council in London, and after many interviews and days of shadowing a social worker at the One Stop Shop for refugees in Brixton (London), she wrote a journal response:

> Before traveling to London, I was under the impression that the biggest problem faced by refugees was political. The only time we hear about refugees is typically when a law is being changed or contested. Sometimes we may hear about how

refugees are draining away tax dollars. We never hear about the hidden psychological trauma experienced by refugees living in our own communities. We never hear about the problems that are not solved by counselors. We never hear the personal stories. When we do, however, we might be open to change. After meeting Pierre, I felt shock, disbelief, anger, and sorrow. The way that refugees are treated needs to be changed. They should no longer be thought of as people who cause problems; in reality, they are the effect of problems. (Quintero, 2014, pp. 32–33)

Educators around the world have been facing similar stark challenges that seem to become only more complex as the months and years proceed. Political and economic conditions affect all aspects of education. In addition, economic globalization—with all its disadvantages and advantages—has uprooted families and brought people together in unpredictable circumstances. Critical theory and critical literacy in research, teaching, and project implementation gets at all these issues in a related way and gets at the most important questions in literacy, learning, teaching, education, and living.

Immigrants are people who move from one country to another for the purpose of permanent residence. A refugee is a person seeking asylum in a foreign country in order to escape persecution. Those who seek refugee status are sometimes known as asylum seekers, and the practice of accepting such refugees is known as offering political asylum. The most common asylum claims in industrialized countries are based upon political or religious grounds. Refugee status may be granted on the basis of the 1951 Convention relating to the Status of Refugees. Refugees are a subgroup of the broader category of displaced persons, and are distinguished from economic migrants, who have left their country of origin for economic reasons, and from internally displaced persons, who have not crossed an international border. Environmental refugees (people displaced because of environmental disasters) are not included in the definition of "refugee" under international law. The practical determination of whether or not a person is a refugee is most often left to certain government agencies within the host countries. This can lead to abuse in a country with a very restrictive official immigration policy. Under the 1951 Convention on Refugees and 1967 Protocol, a nation must grant asylum to refugees, and cannot forcibly return refugees to their nations of origin. However, many nations routinely ignore this treaty (United Nations Higher Commission on Refugees, 2014).

Mary Robinson, former president of Ireland and former director of the United Nations Higher Commission for Human Rights, implores us to "put a human face on migration" (M. Robinson, personal communication,

October 2005). Wisdom and activism sometimes come to us in the smallest and most unexpected ways, through previously silenced yet passionate voices. Interactions with refugee and immigrant families during this research have put a human face on migration for me and the teachers I work with.

Addressing Migrant Issues With Teacher Education Students

It has been documented throughout this book that in the sequence of activities in the classes of early childhood teacher education students spend time and energy on the importance of family history. The premise in critical theory that participants' histories are integral in any educational endeavor is revisited often. Students are asked to reflect and write about how they describe or define their racial or ethnic identities. They are asked to think about what is important and not important to them about this aspect of their identities. They are asked whether their ethnic identities are tied to particular places, and to discuss some of the details of those places that are a part of their lives now, or of memories that are important to them. At the next class session they are asked how they feel about the previous day's work and the homework reflective writing assignment. Many students are excited about the activities, as they provide ways to connect personal experiences to issues we are studying. But not all are happy.

Once, one student said, "I don't like it!" I asked if she would clarify which parts of previous activities she didn't like. She said that she liked the readings, the history field trip, and our previous class discussions. She didn't like the homework reflective writing activity about her family history. She explained,

> My mother tends to live in the present, and you have to get her in a really good state of mind to even hear about things that went on in her past. Most of it is negative stuff anyway, that was used to point out how she had suffered or how "if she had been taught better she would have gone further in life." Such short snippets only served to place upon me a burden which I should but do not want to bear. (Quintero, 2009b, p. 34)

After we listened to this student and critically analyzed her stance, we listened to each other give glimpses into the connection of her comments to some issues of the lives of refugee and immigrant families. We reviewed the important aspect of critical theory that demands that participants' knowledge and opinions be respected and a part of every dialogue and activity. We discussed the complex task of remaining sensitive and creative in our work, because every activity in our work will not be embraced by everyone, and for very good reasons. A focus in the early university classes related to this work, and this study is reading and thinking about what "context" really means to us and to learners we work with.

Another student from the same group, who comes from different life circumstances, asked provocative questions at the end of her reflection:

> I do not recall having any particular conceptions of it [racial identity], and the reason why I say this is because I did not feel disappointment like some immigrants who come to the U.S. and feel as if it was not living up to their preconceived expectations. I did have a picture in mind, but it is hard to put into words. I think that it does not solidify itself until after real-life experience....I am still trying to reconcile what the difference is between personal philosophy, personality, and culture. I find myself making statements about all, after seeing the actions of a few...unable to see, think or believe what is outside of the racial check boxes. Why do we have to check the box? Why are the boxes there in the first place? Who does it benefit?...I feel that the process of migrating, in itself, changes the migrant....The Jamaican culture is neither racial nor ethnic, but it is what I identify with most strongly. Yes, most of the population is Black, and so I guess many of us do not use the Blackness as a unifying factor in the way we view potential friends. It is hard to understand the concept that those identifiers are now used to judge us when we do not necessarily do the same to ourselves. (Quintero, 2009b, p. 36)

I asked whether the class participants saw any connections between this student's story and the stories we might hear from refugees and asylum seekers. A complicated discussion ensued.

One student, commenting on the discussions that day, said:

> Today our group discussion was so informative. It put so much into perspective for me. One connection that jumps out for me is the concept of culture within education. Gonzalez, Moll, & Amanti refer to social theory that legitimized marginalization of minority students by perpetuating an idea of "a culture of poverty," the idea that the culture of the poor (or minorities) was the cause of educational failure. They warn that this theory is flawed because it lacks a holistic approach. This spoke to our discussion of how, as minorities, our family history shaped our college selection process. (Quintero, 2009b, p. 36)

Working With and Learning From Migrant Families and Children

My feelings about the importance of intellectual and inventive capabilities led to my affiliation with critical theory. Critical pedagogists and other postmodern scholars speak often of the importance of educators taking on the risk and responsibility of being intellectual participants. By attending to both the sense of opposition and the sense of engaged participation, intellectuals can explore the possibilities for action. Said (2000) reminds us of the assumption that even though one can't do or know everything, it must always be possible to discern the elements of a struggle or problem dialectically, and that others have a similar stake in a common project. He reminds us that at least since Nietzsche, the writing of history and the accumulations of memory have been regarded in many ways as one of the essential foundations of power.

As explained in earlier chapters, we define critical literacy as using language, both oral and written, as a means of expression, communication, and transformation for ourselves and for those around us. I continually make the case that critical theory, critical literacy, and related approaches to learning about the world and many forms of knowledge can be a potentially effective way to address complexities of our changing world society. A young child labeling a drawing of himself and a friend in both his home language and English, a refugee parent newly arrived in a country demanding that information from her child's school be written in her home language, and a musician using his songwriting and performing talents to address issues of a former life as a child soldier in Africa are all forms of critical literacy that speak truth to power (Quintero, 2009a).

Leila, one of the student teachers working with the Mixtec people in California (discussed in Chapters 2, 3, and 6), wrote in her research journal about initial informal unstructured interview conversations with children from the Mixtec community:

> I had the opportunity to interview and speak with a total of 22 children between the ages of 3 and 5. When I began speaking with them, I asked what their parents or family members do for work. A total of 18 out of 22 children have at least one parent working in agriculture. Of these 18, 13 have both parents working in the agricultural industry. Four of the families that don't have both parents working in agriculture have stay-at-home mothers. Two children noted that their mothers were home because they recently had babies, while one child noted that his mother hurt her foot and another told me that his mom just stays home.

I spoke with several of the children from families who work in agriculture about what they like to do when they are able to spend time with their family. Many children told me that they like to go to Parque de los Patos (the neighborhood park near their school) or to the beach. Some of the children told me about running errands with their parents (grocery store, Walmart, etc.). A few other children told me that they play with their toys when at home. One child said, "Mi mami dame muchas jugetes en casa" (My mom gives me a lot of toys at home).

If I made a book of the observations I took during this work I would title it *Inquisitive Minds*. I was amazed at the things I found! I saw ladybug hunting, finding leaks in hoses, following photo directions, inquiries about print. I was amazed at the variety of interests that varied day by day, week by week, and month by month. What I noticed was that children were deeply involved in their learning and were creating meaning through their work. I think the key to creating activities that are relevant to our families is to make the activity intriguing so that the children can channel and focus on what they need to learn from that particular experience. By using this method, the children are able to cover a variety of content areas, but may also be able to establish a sense of community between home and school. (Quintero, 2012)

I wrote in Chapter 1 and mentioned occasionally the bilingual family literacy project I was involved with years ago, at the beginning of my career. I had practiced listening to children as a preschool teacher, and I learned to listen to families. And I learned what I had suspected but wasn't sure about— that context really matters. The context of the family classes was a planned yet loosely structured group of five families and their children. We planned for five parents and five children. We learned that we often had seven or eight parents (two parents for a few families, or a parent and a grandparent), the kindergarten children from the family (the target group of students of the project), and all the siblings in each family. There were lively groups of up to 25 people with the two facilitators. We also loosely planned (being open for negotiation) for each class to be focused on using Spanish, or focused on using English, or bilingual. We gave parents the choice of which group to go to. Luckily, the groups, reflecting the parents' choices, were pretty equal in terms of numbers. But we quickly realized that parents had chosen their groups based on their previous relationships with one or both of the facilitators, or their relationships with another family in a particular group. Context.

Of course, the other huge lesson for us from that project was how very knowledgeable parents are—from life experiences, some with formal education, and many with only a few years (or none) of education. Of the 11 demonstration projects, we were the only one that implemented the family literacy classes with parents and children participating in the same room, in the same "adjustable" activities, with a mix of English and Spanish, oral language, written language, and bilingual children's literature. And our findings showed this design and context supported literacy in both languages, social and cultural experiences for children and adults, and school achievement as measured in traditional ways (Weinstein-Shr & Quintero, 1994).

Context and Knowledge of Multilingual Educators

We have known for decades the importance of a work force with multilingual and diverse cultural and historical experiences. We know this is important for children who have recently settled in a new country, and yes, more and more, data show that these multilingual educators offer monolingual children positive experiences, new perspectives, and important knowledge and dispositions.

In a collection of autobiographical experiences and family stories of educators (Reyes, 2011), Luis Moll introduces the book with an acknowledgement of the positive impact of the educators' knowledge and dispositions on all students.

> What is also clear in every chapter is the powerful role of emotions in language learning. These two related themes, resilience and emotions—constants in the book and of great theoretical importance in understanding language learning—are easy to miss by those who study only English monolingual development. (Moll, 2011, p. x)

Throughout the autobiographical stories there are a variety of literacy-related ways the families and communities supported the children's biliteracy. Moll (2011) recollects,

> ...I do recall that my early biliteracy was supported almost invisibly...by my father's willingness to buy me comic books in English. He did not care what I was reading, or in which language, as long as I was reading. His intention was, then, not to teach me English, but to get me reading. (Moll, 2011, pp. ix)

Reyes (2011) shares her own story and the variety of meaningful literacy experiences in her home when she was a child:

> Spanish was my mother's only language. Although she never attended school in Mexico, she had been provided a tutor for a few months to teach her to read and write so she was literate in Spanish....[S]he worked cleaning houses all day and

doing laundry for priests at the Cathedral parish. After dinner and a long, hard day, Mamá made time to tell us stories, riddles, and rhymes, and to teach us some songs and games. Her conversations were often peppered with *dichos* or *refranes* (sayings or refrains) to teach us important lessons, or confirm values and attitudes we should inculcate in our behavior. (p. 62)

In Chapter 5, the student teacher Fran wrote in her case study about her personal experience and her work with migrant students. Fran's work resonated with the work of Anzaldúa and her ideas about conocimiento theory. Conocimiento, for Anzaldúa, is an overarching theory of consciousness, comprising

all the dimensions of life, both inner—mental, emotional, instinctive, imaginal, spiritual, bodily realms—and outer—social, political, lived experiences ... the awareness of facultad that sees through all human acts whether of the individual mind and spirit or of the collective, social body. (Hérnandez-Ávila & Anzaldúa, 2000, p. 177–178)

Anzaldúa urged the generation of theories based on those whose knowledges are traditionally excluded from and silenced by academic research. She further asserted that beyond creating theories, "[W]e need to de-academize theory and to connect the community to the academy" (Anzaldúa, 1999, p. xxvi). Anzaldúa (2002) also noted that "Change requires more than words on a page—it takes perseverance, creative ingenuity and acts of love" (p. 574).

Family History and De-Academization of Theory

Through the persona of Fran Martinez, her own historical and cultural influences, and her dedication to working with youth from migrant families, we see illustrations of the de-academization of theory. Multiple examples of conocimiento theory appear as all the dimensions of the lives of migrant students and their tutor interconnect. Martinez has documented memories from her childhood that influenced her strong feelings about her home language, her family, and her passions and interests. These experiences reflect the importance of viewing family, learning, and opportunities through conocimiento theory, and point to her passion for supporting Latino youth from all backgrounds, and especially from migrant families.

Martinez wrote a summary of memories about maintaining home language. When asked what influenced her to nurture and use her home language, complete her education, and persevere in general, she said,

My dad! He always made it a point to (insist that we) keep our Spanish. He would always complain about cousins that spoke Spanish with an accent or didn't know how to conjugate properly while speaking. I definitely have him, and my mom, to thank for my not forgetting Spanish... .

Also, ever since I can remember it was imprinted in my head that not going to college was not an option. It was elementary, middle school, high school, and college. NO OPTIONS! ... And all that is due to my parents. Now that I have moved out and I see the graduation light so close, I definitely have to thank my parents. I appreciate them more now that I am away from them compared to when I saw them every day. (Martinez & Quintero, 2014, p. 206)

In an early childhood teacher education class focusing on methods for teaching multilingual students, Fran wrote an "I Am ..." poem (Christensen, 2003) that reflects conocimiento theory in her own life:

Where I'm From ...
I say I am from a breeze
From a golden globe that warms my every step
From a place where mountains decorate my surroundings
With their white tops on hot summer days
From a place where dreams are supposed to come true
With white picket fences
From a place where people run on their own clock
Places to be and people to see
From a place where gold started it all
And diamonds are a girl's best friend
From a place where stars decorate the floor we walk on
And the stars in the sky hide behind our bright lights

But this is all a lie ...
Where I am really from is from a place full of spirit
And culture is everything
From "Donde esta Fabiola?"
And "Todo el mundo es un coral ... ."
From a place where family is priority
And priority means leaving them behind to better their life
Like my father ...
So now I can say I am from a breeze ... . (Martinez, 2013)

In our work, we use critical theory and critical literacy as processes of both reading history (the world) and creating history. Whose stories are important, and in what ways? In what ways can we learn from the stories? Whose background knowledge will we respect and include, and in what ways? Whose and which knowledge is power, and in what ways? In what ways can we use literacy for specific transformative action? (Quintero, 2009b). The contemporary poet Francisco X. Alarcón asks us if we can "hear the voices between these lines" (Alarcón, 1997, p. 28). Scholars, dedicated teachers, and community activists have documented that many immigrant students come from a variety of backgrounds with different "funds of knowledge" (Moll, Gonzalez, & Amanti, 2005; Steinberg & Kincheloe, 2009) for contributing to our communities and educational programs. Acculturation and language acquisition are impacted by the process of aligning new societal expectations and requirements of immigrants with previous cultural norms, individual perceptions, and experiences preeminent in their lives; yet, these urgent issues are often ignored. It is urgent that university education students learn the complicated practice of recognizing, acknowledging, and incorporating learners' background knowledge while providing them access to new and necessary knowledge for successful participation in the twenty-first century. The research described provides a focus on this work in ways that currently are not often discussed in literature in the field (Martinez & Quintero, 2014).

Martinez explains her work with this group of learners from infant-toddler programs through middle school and high school:

> Working with migrant students ages 3 to 18 has been an experience unlike any other. When I was focusing solely on the younger ages, I had been witness to children struggling to identify a language to speak. What is going to happen to the children when they enter the elementary years and are expected to read a language that no one in their home speaks?

> I am the oldest sibling and from my experiences with younger children, I wonder whom do these kids go to for help? How are parents supposed to be involved parents if this language barrier also stops them? With this, I believe that a well thought out literacy plan will greatly impact these kids and their families. (Martinez & Quintero, 2014, p. 207)

A migrant child in the United States is defined as a child who has parents or guardians who are migratory agricultural workers. Due to this lifestyle, the child is at risk of health problems, poverty, constant relocations, discrimination, and language barriers. The problems can have an intense influence on the educational accomplishments of children of migrant laborers. These are not new elements of struggle to any one of us in this society. Some of these conditions affect many of the poor populations here in the United States.

However, having to constantly move and readjust creates a new set of obstacles and consequences for children and for their education. Migrant students may attend as many as six or seven schools per year (Jachman, 2002).

If we think about conocimiento theory, then we have to really interrupt assumptions about "school readiness" and other stereotypical expectations for performance and narrow approaches to knowledge. Children who are migrating with their families not only are disrupted in the typical school processes and expectations, they also must make new friends and learn to trust again. And some of the children are learning English as a third language. This inconsistency and the many associated challenges set the tone for the child's reading readiness and their ability to retain knowledge, or not.

Another student teacher with an international story and a personal perspective on multilingual issues was Nina. Excerpts from Nina's autobiographical story give more context to the study of curriculum, language, assessment, and webs of other issues.

> To me, being able to speak and understand two or more languages is something I am proud of. It is who I am, part of my identity. As long as I can remember, it is how I grew up. My mother is from the island of Cyprus, and my father, from Lebanon. I remember when I was young, how my mother would often tell me stories in Greek and how my father used to sing me to sleep with his Arabic songs. As I turned 5, we moved to Cyprus for 2 years. I spent the majority of the time visiting my aunts, uncles, cousins, and the rest of my extended family while overseas. We also visited Lebanon, where my uncles, aunts, cousins, and grandparents on my father's side lived. When we came back to the United States, I felt disconnected. I had no family here, so I felt lonely. Also, everyone spoke English. I wanted to hear Greek and Arabic spoken.... Although I could speak and understand English, moving to the U.S. was difficult because I felt I could not relate to anyone.

> We as people are unique in our own way, whether it is in our personalities, opinions, languages or colors. We are cinnamon honey, dark chocolate, raw umber, almond, chestnut, copper, and desert sand. Our colors complement each other, just like a redwood complements a fir tree, or a ladybug complements a grasshopper.

> Although English was my first language, I can understand how dual-language learners feel from an experience I had once. We recently had moved to Lebanon because my father could not find work in Cyprus. We decided to try life in Lebanon. At the time, I was still very young (7–8 years old) and spoke and understood absolutely no Arabic. My parents decided to take me to a school and see how I did the first day. I don't remember much of it, but what I do remember is how lonely I felt. All of the students were laughing and playing and speaking in Arabic. Throughout the day, the teacher never asked me how I was, never mentioned a word in English, nor welcomed me.

I bring up this experience because it is crucial for teachers to understand that they may have students in their classroom that are not fluent English speakers; they cannot just simply sit back and conduct the entire lesson in a language the student is not familiar with....Teachers should remember to be patient and to give students "the gift of time." More time is very important to dual-language learners because it can give them flexibility, allowing them to become more confident and independent, encouraging them to participate in discussions and activities. (Quintero, 2009c)

Teachers From Around the World

As we prepare for our work with families from around the world, the bottom line is that it is important to recognize that many of the teacher education students are also holders of treasures of family history (wonderful and frightening) from their own experiences with migration. I often use a "Where I'm From..." poetry activity to encourage students to think about the importance of their own pasts. They are asked to write about a childhood memory that involves a family (however you define family) celebration involving friends, food, and neighborhood. Then after a few minutes, during the dialogue section of the lesson, the participants discuss their memories with a partner.

Then for the action activity, the participants engage in a "Where I'm From" activity using the following guidelines:

1. Make a list of items found around your home: stacks of newspapers, dirty socks, chewing gum wrappers, etc.
2. Make a list of items found in your yard or outside your apartment.
3. Make a list of items found in your neighborhood.
4. Make a list of relatives' names...especially ones that link you to the past.
5. Make a list of sayings you associate with your family.
6. Make a list of names of foods and dishes that recall family gatherings.
7. Make a list of places where you keep your childhood memories.

   - Discuss your lists
   - Write..."I'm from"...poem
   - Read Around
   - Try it out with children in your classes

A few excerpts from the student teachers' poems show the breadth of personal experience from which they build upon for their in their teaching:

I'm from a small island country.
I'm from Taiwan.
I'm from the delicious Taiwanese food.
Ma Po Tofu, Chow Mein, Spring Roll, Steamed Dumplings
Grandma is good at cooking.
We visited her very often.
I was wondering why Grandma couldn't read the newspaper.
I taught her ㄅㄆㄇㄈ when I was a first grader.
I taught her to write her name 袁黃逢妹.
I was also wondering why Grandma's name has four characters.
She explained that women in her generation have their husband's last name as their
last name.

*****

I am from photo albums filled with memories
of relatives in a far off
distant place.
I am from Gyiagyia's stories and songs
from spanakopita, roast lamb, and cookies
made with love.

I am from a family steeped in culture and traditions
from a people blessed with faith, pride, and love.
I am from hard work and determination,
from struggle and success.
I am from a family of immigrants.

*****

I am from Halmoni, seven eemoes, three samchons, a never ending list of tight knit
cousins, loving parents, a musical family, a happy simple family of three that I now
longingly wish I could have again

I am from the affectionate "mani muk uhs" of eemo and halmoni, "mooh uhs eedun
yul sheem hee hae," "neehahrahwoo" of my halahbuhjee, and my parents comforting
words of "I love you woo ree ddal"

I am from a traditionally rich and historically diverse Korean heritage, from Koguryo
to Shilla Dynasty, Confucian principles, a once oppressed people who rose to become
a globally recognized nation

*****

I am from the, "Ay bendito," "Ave maria"
and "Dios te bendiga hijita" phrases
from mom and dad
phrases I hear when they are happy and mad
I am from the "Si Dios quiere," and "Portate bien"
consejos that are daily reminders of my humble origins
of who I am, where I am from and what I believe. (Quintero, 2009a, pp. 45–46)

References

Alarcón, F. X. (1997). *Laughing tomatoes and other spring poems/Jitomates risueños y otros poemas de primavera*. San Francisco: Children's Book Press.

Anzaldúa, G. (1999). *Borderlands/La frontera: The new mestiza* (2nd ed.). San Francisco: Spinsters/Aunt Lute Press.

Anzaldúa, G. (2002). Now let us shift ... the path of conocimiento ... inner work, public acts. In G. Anzaldúa & A. Keating (Eds.), *This bridge we call home: Radical visions for transformation* (pp. 540–578). New York: Routledge.

Campbell, B. (producer). (2014). Migrants are being deported back to Central America, but their home countries aren't ready for them. PRI's *The World*. Retrieved from http://www.pri.org/stories/2014-08-19/migrants-are-being-deported-back-central-america-their-home-countries-arent-ready

Chishti, M., Hipsman, F., & Bui, B. (2014). Far-reaching implications for broader U.S. immigration debates. *Policy Beat*, Migration Policy Institute. Retrieved from http://www.migrationpolicy.org/article/stalemate-over-unaccompanied-minors-holds-far-reaching-implications-broader-us-immigration

Christensen, L. (2003). *Reading, writing and rising up: Teaching about social justice and the power of the written word*. Milwaukee, WI: Rethinking Schools.

Fujita, A. (2014). Central American kids who make it to the US must cope with the violence they left behind. PRI's *The World*. Retrieved from http://www.pri.org/stories/2014-09-19/central-american-kids-who-make-it-us-must-cope-violence-they-left-behind

Hérnandez-Ávila, I. (2000). Gloria Anzaldúa. In Keating, AnaLouise (Ed.), *Interviews/Intrevistas* (p. 177–194). New York: Routledge.

Jachman, A. (2002). Reading and the migrant student. *SEDL Letter, 14*(3). Retrieved from http://www.sedl.org/pubs/sedl-letter/v14n03/4.html

Martinez, F. A. (2013). FM personal research journal. Unpublished manuscript.

Martinez, F. A., & Quintero, E. P. (2014). Conocimiento: Mixtec youth sin fronteras. In A. Ibrahim & S. Steinberg (Eds.), *The critical youth studies reader* (pp. 205–213). New York: Peter Lang.

Moll, L. C. (2011). Foreword. In M. de la luz Reyes (Ed.), *Words were all we had: Becoming biliterate against the odds* (pp. ix–xi). New York: Teachers College Press.

Moll, L. C., Gonzalez, N., & Amanti, C. (2005). *Funds of knowledge: Theorizing practices in households, communities, and classrooms*. New York: Lawrence Erlbaum Associates.

Penn, H. (2011). *Quality in early childhood services: An international perspective.* Berkshire, UK: Open University Press.

Quintero, E. P. (2009a). *Critical literacy in early childhood education: Artful story and the integrated curriculum.* New York: Peter Lang.

Quintero, E. P. (2009b). *Refugee and immigrant family voices: Experience and education.* Rotterdam, Netherlands: Sense Publishers.

Quintero, E. P. (2009c). Unpublished manuscript.

Quintero, E. P. (2012). Early childhood collaborations: Learning from migrant families and children. In R. Blake & E. Blake (Eds.), *Becoming a teacher: Using narrative as reflective practice* (pp. 168–189). New York: Peter Lang.

Quintero, E. P. (2014). Critical approaches to learning with refugee stories. In E. Quintero & M. K. Rummel (Eds.), *Storying a path to our future: Artful thinking, learning, teaching & research* (pp. 19–34). New York: Peter Lang.

Reyes, M. de la luz (Ed.). (2011). *Words were all we had: Becoming biliterate against the odds.* New York: Teachers College Press.

Said, E. (2000, October 30). The end of Oslo. *The Nation.*

Steinberg, S., & Kincheloe, J. (2009). *Christotainment: Selling Jesus through popular culture.* Boulder, CO: Westview Press.

United Nations Higher Commission on Refugees. (2014). The 1951 refugee convention. Retrieved from http://www.unhcr.org/pages/49da0e466.html

Weinstein-Shr, G., & Quintero, E. P. (Eds.). (1994). *Immigrant learners and their families: Literacy to connect the generations.* Washington, DC: Center for Applied Linguistics, Delta Systems.

· 8 ·

WHAT COULD BE...

Learning From the Tangled Web
of Early Childhood Issues

Mary Catherine Bateson's (2004) reflections on research and work that breaks
new ground always give me guidance when I am concluding a study:

> So many ghosts to be entertained without belief. The ghost at the typewriter or the
> ghostly interlocutor fade, but they have played a crucial role in the formulation of
> thought and the transition to the page. They remain in that place in memory from
> which all of the honored dead speak to enrich our thought, so that even when we
> speak, we echo many voices. (Bateson, 2004, p. 16)

Bateson's (2004) wisdom has guided me for years. The voices I echo are
many—voices in this study, and voices that I have studied from the past.

Another artist scholar, David Romo, has become a guide for me during
previous research endeavors and his advice maintained its relevance for this
study. Romo searched for knowledge and found it through ghosts. Romo
(2005) said of his ghost, "I've been looking for Pancho Villa for the last four
years. I didn't intend to" (p. 3). He began a quest of creating a psychogeog-
raphy of the El Paso, Texas/Juarez, Mexico, border cities. He explained that

he was inspired by the *situationnistes*, an obscure and now-defunct group of French urbanists, artists, and anarchists who, in the 1950s, traveled the streets of Paris noting its various types of ambiance. He thought it was a bit "out there," but the process and intension resonated somehow. So he tried it—not in Paris, but in El Paso, Texas, and Cuidad Juarez, Chihuahua, Mexico, where he had grown up years before. In his resulting book, *Ringside to a Revolution*, he explains:

> *Ringside to a Revolution* deals not so much with history as it does with microhistory....Microhistory at its best is more about small gestures and unexpected details than grand explanations....Ultimately, microhistory is a method of study that focuses more on the mysterious and the poetic than on the schematic. (Romo, 2005, p. 14)

As Romo searched for Pancho Villa's ghost to teach him about the Mexican Revolution, along the way he learned about the important contributions of journalists, *curanderas* (healers), radicals, saints, inventors, jazz musicians, human rights activists in the persona of domestic workers and day laborers, and many others who had important lessons for us all. It is not adequate to study only the ancestry of cultures and ignore how those cultures have evolved and changed through the ages. This complexity of intersections of culture, history (including family history), language, and learning continues to inspire my research with children, families, and teachers that began years ago (Quintero, 2009).

The findings of this current study confirm that an integrated curriculum created collaboratively among teachers, children, families, and community members and critical literacy events strengthen learners' meaningful experiences. Authentic assessment, Storying Learning, documents the cycles of meaning over time. The study points out "more about small gestures and unexpected details than grand explanations," and the children show us how to focus "more on the mysterious and the poetic than on the schematic," to quote Romo, above. The children and their university student teachers do serve as bricoleurs in our research, explaining what we may always understand. And clearly, these findings are influenced by research, policy, issues of equity, and a need for further study and continued research.

In any discussion, academic or political, that I get into about language and languages, I find myself bringing up the work of Gloria Anzaldúa, the writer who published stories, poems, innovative ideas about theory, children's books, and a novel. Because she believed that language and identity are inextricably linked, her writing often is expressed through creative forms of narrative intended to reflect the inclusivity of the *mestiza* identity. She moves between and combines different genres, points of view, and languages. She was storying learning long before we understood that we needed to borrow some of these forms to create authentic assessment. And, while the area of neuroscience is broad and complex, one aspect of this research that is specifically relating to young children's acquisition of language supports the importance of multilingual opportunities for young children (Kuhl & Damasio, 2012; Lin, Imada, & Kuhl, 2011). Furthermore, with new possibilities of Storying Learning we can take some guidance from storytellers and authors who use mixed media to convey information and to document history.

Findings and Hope Through Personal Story and Symbolic Play

Personal story cannot be overrated. We have seen this in our findings about curriculum, assessment, and related issues of policy, access, and funding. A finding that has come up over and over again in this study and through our work is the dynamic way children use personal story in their symbolic and pretend play. When young children dramatize their personal stories through pretend play, topics become layered with the complex issues regarding development and learning that must be discussed and addressed in education. Vivian Paley, during her decades of working with children in Chicago, documented the stories that children tell as part of their play and made the stories part of her daily curriculum. The stories consistently deal with issues of family and community and questions about fairness, justice, and about what it means to be in school (Paley, 1986, 2000). Pretend play is an important facet of young children's lives in terms of cognition, conceptual, and emotional experiences. My own work (Quintero, 2002, 2004, 2009) in many multilingual, multicultural neighborhoods shows that throughout the play and engagement of "pretend" and symbolic story, children have opportunities for language use in home language, target language, and other different forms of language. This language use that evolves naturally and holistically is an integral part of personal and communal story. Family knowledge and literacy are an interwoven fabric of cultural practices. Integrated curriculum, based on critical theory and critical literacy, emphasizing family and cultural story and multicultural children's literature, encourages collaboration and enhances multidirectional participatory learning. We are now certain that teachers and family members must support both the home language and English, or dual-language learners can lose the ability to speak and understand their home language, or lose the balance between the two languages (Castro, Ayankoya, & Kasprzak, 2011).

As I have maintained throughout this study, and as I opened this book saying, early childhood teacher education is about young children's learning, young children's learning to learn, and the social and cultural contexts where this learning takes place. It is also about the people and the human aspects that support this learning. For these reasons, an integrated approach to curriculum is paramount, as is an assessment system that documents the complicated process over time with a collaboration of families, children, teachers, and researchers. We have realized as we have studied the work of New Zealand early care and education researchers and teachers that we can borrow and adapt some of the intellectual, academic, and practice-based structures that they have been using and perfecting for the past decades. These professionals have created a responsive (to children and families, culture and language) and research-based curriculum and an assessment system that is linked foundationally and practically to the curriculum they have created. It is not surprising that the honing in on curriculum and assessment and the tangled web of early childhood issues which must be considered are sometimes overlapping and always influencing each other in one way or many ways. The children guides, our bricoleurs, have illustrated the complexities by way of the case study excerpts.

In Chapter 1 I began from a discouraged place. I recounted that in the United States we gasp with frustration and horror at each policy statement designed to "fix" education, "erase" the achievement gap, and "hold teachers and schools accountable." We know the measures outlined, however well intended, will never work. Our certainty about our stance is for a variety of reasons, and represented by our combined research and varied practice. It is a temptation to identity each point of Race to the Top or each goal and objective from a politician's speech about early care and education and slam the ideas for lack of research, lack of practicality, and their extreme potential for making matters worse. But…we can design, practice, and propose alternatives.

The work with children, families, and dedicated students who are experienced, creative, and courageous about taking risks has provided information and hope...led by the children bricoleurs. We are very serious about children being adept in this capacity as our co-researchers. Throughout the chapters, children taking the research lead as bricoleurs have been introduced. The bricolage creates different ways to read, approach, and use research. The bricolage is a collaboration of children and adults. The children as bricoleurs are not scientists; they are children. In the process of being children they lead and illustrate aspects of their experiences and learning that adult (teachers and parents) researchers pay attention to, support, and analyze.

As this research and the resulting implications have revolved around participatory learner-driven curriculum and assessment, I have taken advice from Pinar concerning the interpretation of the developing work. Pinar (2004) advises: "The complicated conversation that is the curriculum requires interdisciplinary intellectuality, erudition, and self-reflexivity. This is not a recipe for high test scores, but a common faith in the possibility of self-realization and democratization, twin projects of social subjective reconstruction" (p. 8).

Bringing Katherine Nelson (2009) back into the complicated conversation, we heed her warning that "We need to recognize not only that the child is not a machine, but also that *the child is not us*" (p. 7). She continues by suggesting "that instead we turn to the project of acquiring a 'feeling for the organism' in its natural surroundings in the real world, where the organism is the experiencing child" (p. 7).

It is my contention that the children bricoleurs in this study illustrate what Katherine Nelson (2009) says is "...the mind-culture symbiosis" (p. x). She believes "the major breakthrough in human development, in my opinion, the one that made us different from all other animals, was the ability to share subjective meanings" (Nelson, 2009, p. 10). Along these lines, Kuhl (2014) discusses her study of young children's learning language:

> My current working hypothesis is that language learning depends on the social brain. Infants learn not only because they are computational wizards, but also because they are social beings, with a strong drive to communicate from other social beings. (p. 1)

She is one of the cautious yet enthusiastic neuroscientists studying young children. She says,

> My goal is to see in the brain the interaction between brain areas responsible for computation, which are deeply forged in evolution across species, with brain areas that are phylogenetically more modern and enable social understanding. These mechanisms

of social understanding may be at the heart of the interaction I'm talking about. Brain studies will test this hypothesis. (p. 1)

What Could Be....Gearies Primary School

The complex issues unveiled through our study of course raise more questions than answers. In the meantime, we see glimmers of hope and inspiration. The children you will meet in this chapter are discovering creative ways to share their subjective meanings.

Highlighted here is Gearies Primary School, where dedicated teachers, families, and creative children create a path of potential day by day. I was referred to this school in fall 2014. It is located in northeast London, and on a consistent basis, it concretizes some of the new issues in early childhood that collide with established practice. The children and supportive, reflective professionals help the dynamic program illustrate "what can be" in an inspirational way.

The school collaborates on a "statement" about the philosophy of the school and the logistics of how these ideas can be implemented on a day-to-day basis. The school's "statement," including the philosophy and the practicality of implementation, is "dynamic" and always changing. This is, in part, because of the collaboration of all staff, the parents, and the children. Some of the details will be illustrated in this chapter. The school is not perfect; the statement is not a template or a recipe to follow. However, it is presented here to you because as Romo (2005) said, "Microhistory at its best is more about small gestures and unexpected details than grand explanations....Ultimately, microhistory is a method of study that focuses more on the mysterious and the poetic than on the schematic" (p. 14). I believe this excerpt from some of the data from Gearies School is a microhistory of inspirational importance.

It seems important to remember what Peter Moss said in Chapter 6, warning us about "dogma" of agencies and governments approving of a narrow interpretation of curriculum and evaluations for teachers and programs. He cautioned about

> fundamentalist dogma that claims to have the right answer for everything: in short, when neoliberal capitalism becomes a hegemonic system of thought and practice, with its unswerving belief in the virtues of markets and the private, of competition and inequality, and of calculation and individual choice. (2013, p. 191)

I believe through a collaborative research, practice, and professional learning community called the Grants Hill Teaching Alliance and Partnership, the activist teachers and administrators are creating and implementing a more hopeful approach than the dogmatic, hegemonic system Moss warns about above.

I was welcomed to Gearies Primary School, in the London borough of Ilford, in early November 2014. The head teacher, Mr. Robert Drew, sat down with me for a brief orientation. I had previously said that I am especially interested in the programs for the youngest children and also in ways the school is inclusive of the historical and cultural contexts of the families and community. Bob Drew handed me the school's *Early Years Foundation Stage* statement (Gearies Primary School, 2013) and began narrating the school's story.

Mr. Drew (personal communication, November 4, 2014) is very proud and upfront about the fact that Gearies is a teaching school. He explained that Gearies is the only primary school in the borough of Ilford with a specialty of focus on the Early Years. Mr. Drew, who is a longtime resident of the area with experience and knowledge of many other programs, said, "Other schools have no Best Practice meetings; no one is talking about Early Years pedagogy." (Drew, personal communication, November 4, 2014). Gearies does this and much more. Mr. Drew explained that the collaborative professional development is purposefully dynamic and constantly changing according to strengths and needs of the children, individually and collectively. He said, "In our school we view the foundation years (3–5-year-olds) as a basis for all future learning." (Drew, personal communication, November 4, 2014). The school's student population is 3% White (mostly East European immigrants), and 97% are from predominately predominantly Asian and Black communities. Almost all the children are bilingual or learning English as a new language in addition to their home language.

The Early Years in the English education system consists of programs for 3- to 5-year-olds in Foundation Stage classrooms. The 5- to 6-year-olds are in classrooms called "reception classes." The school staff collaboratively created the Gearies Primary School *Early Years Foundation Stage* statement with input from parents and students. It begins with "This statement guides the principles, organisation and provision for learning and teaching in the school's Foundation Stage classrooms" (Gearies Primary School, 2013).

The statement is a concise explanation of rationale, logistics, and acknowledgement of stakeholders. It is reproduced in full here:

How young children learn

"Young children learn by doing. Knowledge is not something that is given to children as though they were empty vessels to be filled. Children acquire knowledge about the physical and social worlds in which they live through playful interaction with objects and people. They are motivated by their own desire to make sense of their world. For children to understand fully and remember what they have learned the information must be meaningful to the child in context of the child's experience and development." (Bredekamp, ed., 1990)

The Early Years Curriculum

Our Early Years Curriculum is based on the revised Early Years Foundation Stage (2012) and is planned to lead smoothly into the National Curriculum at KS1 in a way in which is relevant and meaningful to all children.

Organisation of classes

Our Foundation Stage is divided into nursery and reception classes. Our nursery classes have daily 3 hour morning and afternoon sessions. Each class has 33 children aged between 3 to 4 years with an adult ratio of 1 to 11 (1 qualified teacher and 2 qualified nursery nurses). There are three Reception classes with 30 children each, for children aged between 4 and 5 years old with one qualified teacher always present, and one additional qualified nursery nurse supports the class every morning and some afternoons.

The learning environment

We value a learning environment both inside and outside the classroom, which is carefully organised to enable children to develop and demonstrate characteristics of effective learning. Children are given free access to the outdoor learning space, whenever they are supervised by a member of staff. Adults support children in playing and exploring, active learning and developing creativity and critical thinking. We value resources that promote possibility thinking and offer limitless opportunities for play and learning. Children learn by leading their own play, and by taking part in play that is guided by adults. The child and adult engage in "sustained shared thinking."

Parents as partners

We believe that parents are children's first and most enduring educators and when parents and practitioners work together in Early Years settings, the results have a positive impact on children's development and learning. We encourage parents to contribute to our assessments and provide advice and support on how learning and development can take place at home.

The Key person role

Each child is assigned a key person who helps to ensure that every child's care and learning is tailored to meet their individual needs, to help the child become familiar with the setting, offer a settled relationship for the child and build a relationship with their parents (EYFS, 2012: 3.26).

Planning

Our Early Years planning consists of:

1. **Long term planning** which is based on four EYFS [Early Years Foundation Stage] overarching principles of every child is unique, children learn to be strong and independent through positive relationships, children learn and develop well in enabling environments and children develop and learn in different ways and at different rates. We meet the requirements of the educational programme in relation to the seven areas of Learning and Development, and the characteristics of effective learning.

2. **Medium term planning** informs and helps us focus on short term planning such as planning for continuous provision, planning for outdoor learning and special events and celebrations, planning for identified interests and themes for nursery and reception children. We include a range of experiences and activities appropriate to our groups of children in line with the EYFS education programmes.

3. **Short term planning** provides a weekly overview of teaching and learning activities covering the seven areas of learning and opportunities for the development of the characteristics of effective learning. Short term planning is responsive to individual children's interests and developmental needs.

Observation and assessment

On entry to nursery or reception classes, information is collected from parents to help establish where the child is in relation to the development patterns age-related bands. This information is used as a guide to providing a "best fit" baseline. There are ongoing formative and summative assessments to ensure that practitioners have a clear understanding of a child's progress across all areas of learning and development. Concerns about individual children's progress are identified and addressed. Observations and assessments are kept in an individual child's learning journey, which is available for parents to read and to contribute. In the final term of the year in which the child reaches age five, the EYFS Profile is completed.

Self-help and independence

Through the Early Years, our Practitioners support the children's growing independence and self-help skills. They are positively encouraged to do things for themselves. We support children's growing independence as they do things for themselves, such as dressing and feeding themselves.

Safeguarding

In our school and in our Early Years Provision, safeguarding is a priority. We look to ensure that children feel safe and we aim to promote children's welfare and strive to safeguard children at all times. We look to ensure children's safety, while not unduly inhibiting their risk-taking.

On September 30 to October 1, 2014, Gearies Primary School had their annual inspection visit from Ofsted, the Office for Standards in Education, Children's Services and Skills. Programs for young children and schools are inspected annually in the English education system. Ofsted, which reports directly to Parliament, inspects and regulates services that care for children and young people, and those providing education and skills for learners of all ages (Office for Standards in Education, Children's Services and Skills, 2014).

The inspectors were pleased and impressed with what they saw. The school staff insisted upon keeping to their daily routine, demonstrating the integrity of work they always strive for—as opposed to preparing for the evaluation visit with a "performance" of sorts. An excerpt from the Ofsted report noted that:

The early years provision is Outstanding

- Children make outstanding progress because of precise, responsive planning for their individual needs. This is coupled with the provision of imaginative resources and creative use of spaces. By the end of the Reception year nearly all children have reached a good level of development.
- Staff place a strong emphasis on helping children learn how to get along with one another. They take the necessary steps to keep children safe and understand procedures intended to promote safeguarding.
- Adults use talk very skillfully to promote rapid learning of phonics (the sounds that letters make).
- Children benefit from a very effective balance of working directly with an adult and time to explore on their own or with their classmates.
- The early years leader has an extensive knowledge of every child in the setting. He uses this to ensure all staff plan learning opportunities that meet children's individual needs. (Gearies Primary School, 2014)

Dan Lea's Research and Shared Findings

Bob Drew explained that they have many master's-level teachers and teachers currently studying for their master's degree at Gearies Primary School. He also emphasized that in their collaborative professional development meetings the school always uses the master's work of the teachers to further understand the children, the context, and their practice. An example of this sincere respect for colleagues' work shines through in the example of the deputy head's master's research study of dramatic play of a group of children in the Early Years cohort.

The deputy head teacher at Gearies Primary School is Mr. Dan Lea. Mr. Lea had recently finished his master's study, which culminated in an ethnographic study of how children in the reception cohort (4- and 5-year-olds) of Gearies Primary School use fantasy violence in their play. Mr. Lea spent time with me sharing his research and explaining connections of his research project to the work with the children on a day-to-day basis. As he planned, designed, and implemented his qualitative study, he shared his thinking with his colleagues at the school and with the children. The ethnography format was an effective way to capture the context of the school and to delve into the multiple layers of issues involved in children's fantasy play.

Mr. Lea's data are full of detail and meaning that is impossible to fully include in this brief chapter. Yet, considering my wish to highlight a program for young learners that offers hope and practical day-to-day information about how to provide responsive, critical reflective practice in early childhood, I was thrilled to be invited to visit the school and to begin learning about how they do what they do. Furthermore, as is often (or always) the case in early childhood agendas, so many of our important issues overlap and are webs of complicated, connected influence.

Not only were Bob Drew and Dan Lea willing to spend time, conversation, and shared reflections with me while I was there, they also remained willing to review by email the excerpts from their data that they shared with me as I included them in this chapter. I have cited Mr. Lea's unpublished research journal as Lea, 2012a, and his thesis notes, an unpublished manuscript, as Lea, 2012b. While I have been able to include only small excerpts from these documents, I have tried to maintain the flavor of the context of the school, the relationships among adults and children, and the integrity of the work by including some long quotes that bring in important contextual details and the actual comments of the participants.

Mr. Lea is a leader in a school that is responsive to diverse learners from all over the world. The school is based upon and organized around a collaborative model that Bob Drew, the head teacher, and Dan Lea shepherd through on good days and difficult days; all school policies are inclusive of family engagement. So, please, see some glimpses into aspects of these complexities as you read about through just a fraction of the work Mr. Lea, the children of Gearies, and the staff have been involved in.

In terms of demographics, Mr. Lea reported that the school is a larger-than-average-sized infant (Early Years) school. The overwhelming majority of the pupils are of minority ethnic backgrounds, and more than three-quarters of learners are new to the English language or bilingual. There is a steady increase in Eastern European families and refugees. He reported that in preparation for finalizing the focus of his research study, he was moved by the following data:

> The data collected in our March 2012 pupil conferences identified that 22% of the children felt the adults in the school didn't always listen to them, monitoring reports identified a need for the early years team to improve their ability to engage

in the children's autonomously created play, and the children's creative development attainment scores were lower than expected. (Lea, 2012b, p. 8)

Specifically, Lea's ethnography aimed "to identify how the children in this reception cohort use fantasy violence [play] to support their learning" (Lea, 2012a, p. 10).

His research questions were:

1) How do the children in the reception cohort of a suburban London school use fantasy violence in their play?
2) What are the barriers that stop the adult practitioners working in this early years team from engaging with the children in their autonomously selected play choices? (Lea, 2012b, p. 10)

Research Frame for Lea's Study

Lea (2012b) framed some of his research around the work of Garrick, Bath, Dunn, Maconochie, Willis, and Wolstenholme (2010), who found that when children had the opportunity to engage in activities with unlimited time in which to develop their autonomous play, they often demonstrated high levels of creativity and a wider range of multiple interests and more complex play, sustained their engagement in the learning for significantly longer periods of time, and were distinctively more involved in planning their learning with a practitioner who promoted the child's interests.

In the conclusion of the Garrick et al. (2010) report it, is noted:

1) Although many of the findings reported here are consistent with themes, commitments and guidance in Early Years Foundational Stage, it was also clear that there are omissions in the Early Years Foundational Stage, in part due to the emphasis on children as receivers of a curriculum generated by adults (p. 35).
2) As highlighted by United Nations General Comment 7 (United Nations Committee, 2005), children have the right to express their views about "the development of policies and services," and staff should recognize the expert contribution children can make. (p. 35)

Lea (2012b) reported that in the Early Years Foundational Stage settings he participated in for his study, the children said over and over again that adults did not accept all of their play choices. He contends that Garrick et al. (2010) place the historical literature of Erikson (1950), Bronfenbrenner (1979), and Bettelheim (1987) into a modern context. This work identifies also that free, autonomous play choice supported by flexible resources promotes the most innovative and sustained experiences of play.

In establishing the importance of children's autonomy over play choice, Lea (2012b) cites Moss (2008), who is dismayed by trends in educational policy and says "All the talk is on 'meeting potential.' It seems to me that we don't allow any possibility of new things happening" (Moss, 2008, p. 11). In spite of literature providing evidence that play is key to physical, mental, and social well-being (Bruce, 2006; Paley, 1988; Pellegrini & Smith, 1998), there is evidence that less and less of children's time is devoted to play.

Regarding the issue of violence in pretend play, Holland (2003) points out that the validity of some studies (Sutton-Smith, 1999; Watson & Peng, 1992) is flawed because there was no distinction made between "play fighting" and "actual aggressive behavior," and that the actual incidents of antisocial behavior recorded by those with a preoccupation with play themes around weapons, war, and superheroes was not statistically significant. Jarvis (2010) contends that fantasy violence, or rough-and-tumble play, is nonviolent, since such play seems to only occur between friends, with the actual moments of physical contact controlled by the children themselves, which is different by definition to moments of real aggression. The distinctions Jarvis (2010), Grossman (2008), and Katch (2002) make between play and actual aggression are fundamental definitions to use in challenging adult perceptions related to the value of fantasy violence play (Lea, 2012a).

Design Decisions With Collaboration of Teachers and Children

As previously explained, Lea shared his ongoing ethnographic research with colleagues in school meetings. He cited Olusoga (2008) when reflecting on some of this own observations of the discrepancies in adults' reactions to boys' play versus girls' play. Lea explains,

> The boys were simply playing dragons, chasing, catching, imprisoning each other in imaginary caves, laughing, collectively swapping roles, while the teacher observing was ready to stop the play at any sign of physical contact. But the contact in this play was non-aggressive when they were taking each other to imaginary prisons, which were some pieces of material over some barrels. They supported each

other, two children escorting a captured dragon by each arm, but the play was stopped [by the teachers] and the group sent away. (Lea, 2012a, p. 4)

Lea continues,

> At the same time, Javeen[1] had been creating the role of dragon catchers, taping yogurt pots onto sticks, helped by adults, to make nets and dragon cages. These were then used to chase and actually hit boys on their backs in an attempt to capture them. This play was non-aggressive also, but celebrated as play that improved the children's self esteem, seen as empowering and imaginative. Even when at one point where as self-appointed queen, Javeen aggressively declared, "The boy dragons would all be in prison in the caves and killed." There was no reaction from observing practitioners, no stopping of the play. (Lea, 2012a, p. 4)

Interestingly, Lea (2012b) notes that Olusoga (2008) highlights examples of child play and adults' reactions and states that these incidents illustrate a double standard about how adult females' perceptions relate to rough-and-tumble play. Yet, Lea says,

> In my experience I'm not too sure this is a gender related issue or more to do with what seems to be a generically adopted default setting when observing rough, fantasy violence play created by boys. As adults we think that the boys do it just to be rough and physical. Yet, when girls engage in such imaginative play, we view it as empowering, an expression of developing self-confidence. (Lea, 2012b, p. 5)

After observing the boys' and girls' play and the differing adult reactions to that play, Lea began to be curious about the actual value of fantasy violence play and how children in the reception cohort use make-believe violence in their play and how these choices are perceived by practitioners. He cites Jarvis (2007), raising the issue that play valued by children becomes invisible to the adult because the adult is only observing the play from the viewpoint of ensuring the play is safe. The adult's ability to engage in the play is restricted by a sense of stress relating to the play becoming dangerous and any resulting accidents being attributed to their failure to ensure safe play. The adult is primarily concerned with safety, ensuring no accidents occur and therefore avoiding the possibility of parental complaints. This leads to "stressful surveillance" and limited interaction, and the child-valued play becoming invisible.

In a related incident, Lea explains the play of Arun and two friends, who used small Legos to make "sprayers" to kill dragons and other things, because the teachers don't like them making "guns." The boys make the sprayers and use them mostly on the furthest side of the outside area so they are less likely to be seen by the teachers. Arun said, in answer to a question about where they play, "in the big playground. When we go there the teacher can't see us. If the teachers are not around, we are playing guns....I like playing guns." Lea asks, "I still don't get the rule; you can shoot in the face, but not use big Legos?" Arun answers, "Teachers don't get it. It's only pretend. You can shoot in the face. It's not real, but you can't make things with big Legos. I can make what I need quickly with little Legos" (Lea, 2012a, p. 11). Lea (2012a) reflects,

> It is my responsibility, as it is of any teacher, to use this observed information to challenge misconceptions by adults about Arun's learning and behavior, and ultimately, it is my responsibility, as it is his class teachers', to use these observations of the child's skills to support my engagement with Arun to help him realise the potential he has to be successful, to challenge moments when he seems disengaged, to ensure as an educator creating a learning around these children, [that] each child has the opportunity to reach their full potential to enjoy experiencing success which is celebrated. (p. 13)

Lea (2012a), after much thought and consideration, reported as he began to implement his actual study,

> I have decided that in this enquiry I shall adopt the role of a full participant due to the advantage that I have in being so connected to the everyday lives of the children....The children will be told why we are involved in the project and what we hope to achieve, with the children and their parents informed that I am acting as a researcher studying this particular group. (p. 19)

Mr. Lea respected the opinions of the children and had a commitment to collaborating with them, rather than just studying them. Lea (2012a) writes:

> There is a consensus in this literature that ethnographic researchers should actively seek to include children's viewpoints in their ethnographical research, especially focusing on how the children in such research link their perceptions and interpretations arising from their social world to the way in which they and others learn. (p. 35)

Implementing Lea's Study at Gearies

Importantly, Lea asks:

> If all of these different research studies cited by Jarvis (2010) draw the conclusion that as humans we have a biological blueprint to learn, and within this capacity for learning there exists a possible biological and cultural preference for very social, rough-and-tumble play, what limitations to the learning experiences of children

preoccupied with fantasy violence and rough-and-tumble play do we create when we fail to recognize, engage in, or value their play; how do we see what's really happening? If the real narrative of the play is hidden, ignored, or dismissed, and with it, its importance to the child's learning? (2012a, p. 22)

Intentionally, we go back to the quote by Nelson (2009) from Chapter 5:

Meaning is in the mind and the brain; it is also in the body that recognizes familiar things and places. Meaning comes to reside in the child, but it also resides in the social world, in the affect-laden interactions with caretakers and others, in the symbols and artifacts of the culture, in the language spoken around the child. (p. 10)

In another incident recorded in Lea's research journal (2012a) regarding the social emotional importance of pretend play, he recounts an incident involving Dane, one of Arun's best friends:

Today he seemed very quiet and withdrawn from his friends. As I joined the group on the carpet and asked what was wrong, Arun told me that Dane's house had been burgled. I asked Dane if he wanted to talk about this if this was upsetting him. He began retelling how he had been woken up to his Mum screaming and how had had seen the burglars.

"In my house we were all asleep and the downstairs alarm went and my Mum said there's a burglar in the house and my sister screamed and was crying...." (Lea, 2012a, p. 23)

At this point Arun put his arm around Dane and continued Dane's story for him—"Yeah then you did a flip and got your laser guns and killed them" (Lea, 2012a, p. 23)—explaining how Dane had then somersaulted over the stairs, had taken out his laser guns and swords and killed the burglars. Then he said that hundreds more came up the stairs, but Dane was too strong for them all, and he used his Power Ranger skills to kill them all:

We got some more guns and lizards and we kept shooting and there were so many burglars and we got all our guns and swords and fighted (sic) them and there was blood and we killed them all and a big momma came in a car with the police and they came and helped us. (Lea, 2012a, p. 23)

Lea (2012a) noted then,

Dane's appearance instantly changed. He joined Arun, all smiles, on the carpet to act out his slaying of the burglars through a range of staged rolls, dives, and pretend fight scenes. After this short play, Dane sat back down with me, told me he felt better and that his Mum loved him and wouldn't let anyone hurt him. (p. 23)

Selected Findings From the Gearies School Context

As previously mentioned, Lea did find this aspect of violence in play important, and spent considerable time observing, playing with, and talking with Arun and his friends. Lea (2012a) wrote

> Arun is a 5-year-old child in our reception year group. I have been supporting this year's group practitioners in examining not only how well they play with children but also to what extent they are effective in creating learning opportunities in which shared sustained thinking occurs Siraj-Blatchford & Sylva (2004) refer to shared sustained thinking as a learning experience in which two or more individuals "work together" in an intellectual way to solve a problem, to clarify a concept, evaluate activities, or extend a play narrative.

> As part of this initiative, I have spent a substantial amount of my time developing this shared sustained thinking experience with Arun and his friends. During this time it was clear to me that Arun was a confident and influential figure in his peer group. Many of the other boys would follow his play narratives, agree to changes to the play that he instigated, copy his actions, and even, during a rain storm, style their hair in a similar way to his. When observing Arun and his friends engaged in their most favourite play choice, fantasy violence, it was clear that under his supervision the group would consistently create socio-dramatic play of a high quality.

> What became most apparent was that Arun was a leader who also used his observations of adults to ensure he and his friends could still engage in banned make-believe violence play, unnoticed. On one occasion when visiting his classroom, I observed how before Arun and his group noticed me they were completely engaged in some kind of make-believe weapon play. On spotting me they stopped, sticks behind their backs. Arun commented, "It's all right, he lets us play." I asked him what he meant, and he replied, "She doesn't let us play, the teacher, but you do." After Arun announced this, the group continued in their game, Dragon killing, a favourite we had invented together the week before.

> Arun's teacher came over, asking about our conversation. I shared our chat with her and she replied, "Really, I always thought he was quiet, not very clever, not really wanting to do anything apart from mess about with Dane." I invited his teacher to sit and watch the group play. During this time Arun invented the group's play narrative, shared innovative ideas and creative language, and ensured that their play remained in a space away from other teachers' observations. He negotiated arguments over narrative development to a compromised conclusion and stopped the play when a

peer fell over, to make sure he wasn't hurt. Arun's teacher watched, and then commented, "I got him wrong." (Lea, 2012a, p. 37)

In these sessions, Lea (2012a) reflects on three thoughts:

1. The children seemed to find it difficult to play inside, almost as if their creative narratives and play innovations were in some way restricted by being in the "classroom," a space designed and governed by teachers and adults for the children's involvement in directed learning.
2. Props are important.
3. Once outside, [when] the children have the space they need to move away from direct adult surveillance, regulation, their creative narratives return and their play is notably more innovative. (p. 42)

Further Selected Findings Relating to Family Engagement

Lea's research is rich as it relates to many specific issues about pretend play in groups. A related type of creativity and imagination that children exhibit is that of connecting activities from school with activities at home. Lea (2012a) reported that as a school, they regularly send out creative and innovative home learning projects based on observations of what the children have enjoyed during the week. One week, while playing with the children, he made himself a superhero costume from an old blanket. He said, "The group loved the idea of making costumes, so we all made some improvised outfits from materials, blankets, felt pens, glue and paper" (p. 54). Lea decided to ask the teachers if that week, as part of their home learning, a flyer could be sent out asking parents to help their children make a homemade superhero outfit. They agreed. He reported,

> Normally, our most dedicated families, on average, four families per class only, engage in any kind of creative or innovative home learning activity. However, in response to this flyer, on average, 28 out of the 30 children in each of the three classes returned to school on the Monday with their homemade outfits.

> One parent shared with me how her daughter, "Star Girl," insisted all weekend that she needed a costume, to the point where Mum found herself stitching a cap at 11pm on Sunday evening. (Lea, 2012a, p. 55)

A more specific way an individual child was affected by this small project is seen in an excerpt from a case study of Rana. Lea (2012a) writes,

Rana is a child who has a poor self-image. When asked what she is good at, she often replies, nothing. Her mum and dad have separated and her home life is split between her two new families. She spends alternate weeks with Dad, stepmother, and stepfamily, and with Mum and her three sisters and brother. On occasions her parents have been warned by staff about inappropriate ways in which they discipline the children.

During the homemade heroes project, Rana's whole self-image and learning disposition/attitude to school completely changed. During this project she created an amazing costume, participated in collaborative superhero play in the garden, and just generally seemed a much more confident, happy child. At the end of the week both her mum and dad came in to talk to her teacher about the confidence she had shown at home, how each evening she would talk about what was happening at school, ask Mum to help with her costume, and get up early to be ready for school. (pp. 56–57)

And, So What? Implications and Hope

What does this have to do with learning in early childhood and to living together in the twenty-first century? Bateson (2004) guides us to look beyond the surface differences.

Beyond focused expertise, it is still possible to trace similarities between, say, the degradation of a forest biome and the decay of an urban neighborhood. Analogies from one person's experience to another's are often linked through the characteristics that all humans share: our bodies, of dependent beginnings, our growth through multiple states, our learning and our dying. (Bateson, 2004, p. 4)

We do learn from each other's experiences. We learn from children. We learn from colleagues we have yet to meet.

Finally, I would like to bring in wisdom I seem to refer to with every new group of teacher education students. An artist, political activist, and storyteller helps frame the gargantuan nature of our work and offers advice. Ortiz (2001) recounts a history of indigenous people in Mexico and explains that for 500 years the people have been living a history of questions, a history in which folktales and art are the ways indigenous people speak truth to power. In *The Story of Questions* the conversation between Subcomandante Marcos and the elder Antonio is about Zapata, a leader of the Mexican Revolution who was of indigenous ancestry and spoke Nahuatl. Ortiz says, "But it is also not about Zapata. It is about what shall happen. It is about what shall be done" (Ortiz, 2001, p. 51). The folktale ends thus:

This is how the true men and women learned that questions are for walking, not for just standing around and doing nothing. And since then, when true men and women want to walk, they ask questions. When they want to arrive, they take leave. And when they want to leave, they say hello. They are never still. (p. 51).

May we never be still.

Note

1. Names changed to protect privacy.

References

Bateson, M. C. (2004). *Willing to learn: Passages of personal discovery*. New York: Steerforth.

Bettelheim, B. (1987, March 1). The importance of play. *The Atlantic*. Retrieved from http://www.theatlantic.com/magazine/archive/1987/03/the-importance-of-play/305129/

Bronfenbrenner, U. (1979). *The ecology of human development: Experiments by nature and design*. Cambridge, MA: Harvard University Pres.

Bruce, T. (2006). *Early childhood: A guide for students*. London: Sage.

Castro, D. C., Ayankoya, B., & Kasprzak, C. (2011). *New voices/Nuevas voces: Guide to cultural and linguistic diversity in early childhood*. Baltimore: Brookes.

Erikson, E. (1950). *Childhood and society*. New York: Norton.

Garrick, R., Bath, C., Dunn, K., Maconochie, H., Willis, B., & Wolstenholme, C. (2010). *Children's experience of the early years foundation stage*. Research Report DFE-RR07. Sheffield, UK: Sheffield Hallam University, Centre for Inclusion Research.

Gearies Primary School. (2014) Ofsted Inspection 30 September to 1 October. Extract from the Report.

Gearies Primary School. (2013). *Early Years Foundation Stage*. Retrieved from http://www.geariesprimaryschool.co.uk/the-early-years-foundation-stage/

Grossman, S. (2008). Offering children choices: Encouraging autonomy and learning while minimizing conflicts. *Early Childhood News*. Retrieved from http://www.earlychildhoodnews.com/earlychildhood/article_view.aspx?ArticleID=607

Holland, P. (2003). *We don't play with guns here: War weapons and superhero play in the early years*. Maidenhead, UK: Open University Press, McGraw-Hill Education.

Jarvis, P. (2007). Monsters, magic, and Mr. Psycho: Rough and tumble play in the early years of primary school. *Gender and Education 7*(1), 69–87.

Jarvis, P. (2010). Born to play: The biocultural roots of rough and tumble play, and its impact upon young children's learning and development. In P. Broadhead, J. Howard, & E. Wood (Eds.), *Playing and learning in the early years: From research to practice* (pp. 61–78). London: Routledge

Katch, J. (2002). *Under deadman's skin: Discovering the meaning of children's violent play*. Boston: Beacon Press.

Kuhl, P. (2014, January). How babies learn language: Q&A with Patricia Kuhl. *Cognitive Neuroscience Blog Archive*. Retrieved from https://www.cogneurosociety.org/cns-2014-blog-coverage/

Kuhl, P. K., & Damasio, A. (2012). Language. In E. R. Kandel, J. H. Schwartz, T. M. Jessell, S. Siegelbaum, & J. Hudspeth (Eds.), *Principles of neural science* (5th ed.) (pp. 1353–1372). New York: McGraw-Hill

Lea, D. (2012a). *An ethnographic study of how children in the receptions cohort of a suburban London school use fantasy violence in their play* (Unpublished research journal). Ilford, U.K.

Lea, D. (2012b). *An ethnographic study of how children in the receptions cohort of a suburban London school use fantasy violence in their play* (Unpublished thesis notes). Ilford, U.K.

Lin, J.-F. L., Imada, T., & Kuhl, P. K. (2011). Mental addition in bilinguals: An fMRI study of task-related and performance-related activation. *Cerebral Cortex, 22*(8), 1851–1861.

Moss, P. (2013). Need markets be the only show in town? In E. Lloyd & H. Penn (Eds.), *Childcare markets: Can they deliver an equitable service?* (pp. 191–208). Bristol, UK: Policy Press.

Moss, P. (2008). *Markets and democratic experimentalism: Two models for early childhood education and care*. Gütersloh: Bertelsmann-Stiftung. Retrieved from http://www.bertelsmann-stiftung.de/bst/de/media/xcms_bst_dms_24015__2.pdf [43 s]

Nelson, K. (2009) *Young minds in social worlds: Experience, meaning and memory*. Cambridge, MA: Harvard University Press.

Office for Standards in Education, Children's Services and Skills. (2014). About us. Retrieved from http://www.ofsted.gov.uk/about-us/who-we-are-and-what-we-do/services-we-inspect-or-regulate

Olusoga, P. (2008). We don't play like that here. In A. Brock, S. Dodds, P. Jarvis, & P. Olusoga (Eds.), *Perspectives on play* (pp. 40–64). Harlow, UK: Pearson.

Ortiz, S. (2001). Haah-ah, mah-eemah, Yes, it's the very truth. In Subcomandante Marcos, *Questions and swords: Folktales of the Zapatista revolution, as told by Subcomandante Marcos* (pp. 50–59). El Paso, TX: Cinco Puntos Press.

Paley, V. G. (1986). *Boys and girls: Superheroes in the doll corner*. Chicago: University of Chicago Press.

Paley, V. G. (1988). *Bad guys don't have birthdays: Fantasy play at four*. Chicago: University of Chicago Press.

Paley, V. G. (2000). *White teacher*. Cambridge, MA: Harvard University Press.

Pellegrini, A., & Smith, P. (1998). Physical activity play: The nature and function of a neglected aspect of play. *Child Development, 68*, 577–598.

Pinar, W. (2004). *What is curriculum theory?* Mahwah, NJ: Lawrence Erlbaum. Associates.

Quintero, E. P. (2002). A problem-posing approach to using native language writing in English literacy instruction. In S. Ransdell & M. L. Barbier (Eds.), *Psycholinguistic approaches to understanding second language writing* (pp. 34–46). Amsterdam: Kluwer Press.[

Quintero, E. P. (2004). *Problem-posing with multicultural children's literature: Developing critical, early childhood curricula*. New York: Peter Lang.

Quintero, E. P. (2009). *Critical literacy in early childhood education: Artful story and the integrated curriculum*. New York: Peter Lang.

Romo, D. D. (2005). *Ringside seat to a revolution: An underground cultural history of El Paso and Juarez—1893–1923.* El Paso, TX: Cinco Puntos Press.

Siraj-Blatchford, I., & Sylva, K. (2004). Researching pedagogy in English pre-schools. *British Educational Research Journal, 30*(5), 713–730.

Sutton-Smith, B. (1999). Evolving a consilience of play definitions: Playfully. *Play and Culture Studies, 2,* 239–258.

United Nations Committee on the Rights of the Child. (2005). *General comment no. 7: Implementing child rights in early childhood.* Geneva, Switzerland: Author. Retrieved from http://www2.ohchr.org/english/bodies/crc/docs/.../GeneralComment7Rev1.pdf

Watson, M. W., & Peng, Y. (1992). The relation between toy gun play and children's aggressive behavior. *Early Education and Development, 3*(4), 370–389.

RETHINKING CHILDHOOD

GAILE S. CANNELLA, *General Editor*

Researchers in a range of fields have acknowledged that childhood is a construct emerging from modernist perspectives that have not always benefited those who are younger. The purpose of the Rethinking Childhood Series is to provide a critical location for scholarship that challenges the universalization of childhood and introduces new, reconceptualized, and critical spaces from which opportunities and possibilities are generated for children. Diverse histories and cultures are considered of major importance as well as issues of critical social justice.

We are particularly interested in manuscripts that provide insight into the contemporary neoliberal conditions experienced by those who are labeled "children" as well as authored and edited volumes that illustrate life and educational experiences that challenge present conditions. Rethinking childhood work related to critical education and care, childhood public policy, family and community voices, and critical social activism is encouraged.

For more information about this series or for submission of manuscripts, please contact:

> Gaile S. Cannella
> gaile.cannella@gmail.com

To order other books in this series, please contact our Customer Service Department at:

> (800) 770-LANG (within the U.S.)
> (212) 647-7706 (outside the U.S.)
> (212) 647-7707 FAX

Or browse online by series at:
> www.peterlang.com